Where is your Lig

Jörg W. Knoblauch, Johannes Hüger, Marcus Mockler

Where is your Lighthouse?

Navigate your life and take charge of your own future

Illustrations by Werner Tiki Küstenmacher

First published in German as *Dem Leben Richtung geben: In drei Schritten zu einer selbstbestimmten Zukunft* by Campus Verlag, Frankfurt/Main, 2003

This translation first published in Great Britain in 2005 by
Cyan/Campus Books, an imprint of

Cyan Communications Limited
4.3 The Ziggurat
60–66 Saffron Hill
London EC1N 8QX
www.cyanbooks.com

A CIP record for this book is available from the British Library

ISBN 1-904879-10-1

Translated and typeset by Cambridge Publishing Management
(Translators: Richard Elliott and Martin Pearce)

Printed and bound in Great Britain by
TJ International, Padstow, Cornwall

Contents

Foreword

This book is about nothing less than your life. Do you like getting up in the morning? Do you enjoy your job? Is your leisure time relaxing and stimulating? Is your family life happy? Are you living your dream? Or is life passing you by while you do a job you don't like, one that leaves you hardly any time to unwind or enjoy personal relationships? You have a choice.

Escape stress and the treadmill of everyday life and embark upon a journey of discovery into the most fascinating thing in the world: yourself. Get to know your true abilities, your uniqueness and your inner self and lead the life you have always dreamed of leading. Along the way you'll acquire greater calm and greater control.

I want you to be able to say to yourself each evening: "I couldn't have had a more fulfilling day." This, however, requires a certain effort on your part. If you want to give your professional and private life a new direction, you will have to develop new habits concerning the way you view your potential and handle your time and will need to internalize new ways of thinking.

This motivational book is based on countless in-house counseling sessions and seminars. Its color derives from encounters with a diverse range of people and their life stories. Thanks to the practical instructions given on the following pages, all these individuals have become more relaxed, more satisfied and happier. Why don't you take that first, decisive step? – there's no time like *today*.

Professor Dr. Lothar J. Seiwert, co-author of the international bestseller, *How to Simplify your Life*.

Life in the hamster wheel

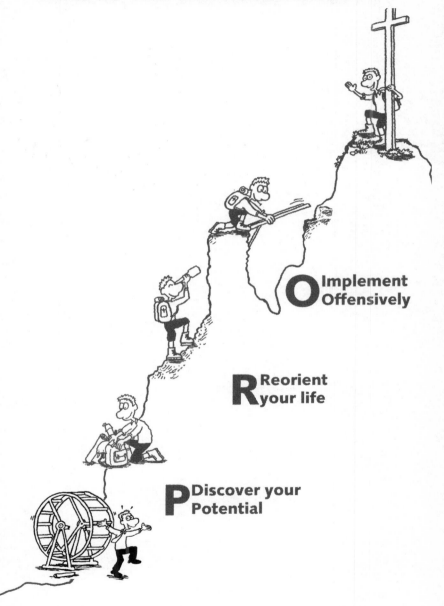

You cannot lengthen your life or broaden it,
you can only deepen it.

Gorch Foch

The caller was actually in an enviable position: he had worked his way to the top, had a fantastic income and really couldn't complain about his professional life or financial situation. He summed up his reasons for requesting a counseling session with us in a single, shattering sentence:

"I've made a million – but I haven't yet lived."

Only a minority of this book's readers will be in the millionaire category, but nearly everyone faces the same problem. We go all out for more money, a better career, greater influence and greater security, only to realize one day: "I haven't yet lived."

We live in an age that seems to be losing its optimism. Many of us feel trapped, weighed down by worries about work prospects, the threat of unemployment, increasing competition and the pressure of deadlines. In many areas, the time when ideas and visions could be pursued is long gone and in some industries the name of the game is now survival. This is reflected in workload – not only of managers but of many other employees too. The eternal question of whether there is life after death has taken a surprising twist. The question now is: is there life *before* death?

And life is what this book is all about. Our life is like a ship that occasionally sails into rough waters. It is difficult to maintain our course in a storm. Anyone can lose their bearings temporarily – when the coast and its life-preserving lighthouse disappear from view or when modern navigation systems fail. This leaves us at the mercy of the waves. Will we be able to find our bearings again, to reset our compass, to harness favorable winds? In short, will we be able to reorient our life?

This book will provide you with the necessary tools to do this. In their seminars, the authors have come to the assistance of numerous men and women who have found themselves "adrift on the high seas." Not only those caught in the eye of the storm, but also those sailing calmer waters who wanted to gather speed and steer a more direct course for their goals in life. Everyone is overcome at some stage in life by the feeling that they have drifted off course. Using the three-stage plan to which we wish to introduce you in this book, you will quickly regain a clear view of your own lighthouse and learn the best way of attaining your true destination. This plan is encapsulated in the *PRO formula*:

Discover your Potential. The first stage will focus on the true you. What are your characteristics? Who are you? What's inside you? You will come to realize what an extraordinary wealth of gifts and qualifications you have for your journey through life and to identify your heart's true desires.

Reorient your Life. In the second stage we will help you give your life direction. We humans possess the unique capacity to think creatively about our future and to shape it consciously. Building on what you have learned during the first stage, you will work out the goals that make your life worth living – the goals that prevent you from drifting off course.

Implement Offensively. It is not enough for your navigational chart, the route to your lighthouse, only to exist in your head or on paper. It must be lived. You will be given the necessary tools to get your ship underway. The world is full of educated failures, people who have enormous knowledge but don't know how to use it. This third stage will show you how to move from knowing to acting. After all, you can't reap what you don't sow.

We are delighted you want to give your life a new direction. The methods in this book have been tried and tested – by the seminar participants, and also by the authors. Many examples used in the individual chapters are drawn directly from this experience. As is usual in books, these examples and experiences have been simplified or modified slightly. In order not to overcomplicate the examples, we have chosen not to identify which author contributed a particular case. For all of us stand by each of the statements made.

How then to get the most out of this book? The most important thing is not only to read each chapter carefully but also to work through all the workshops. This will enable you to arrive at a proper realization of what makes up your life. You will discover hidden aspects of your life that you have always neglected as a result of external pressures. Some of the workshops take the form of tests with boxes to tick, others require more detailed answers. If at any point you find that this book does not provide you with enough space, don't be afraid to make extra notes elsewhere. You might even want to start a notebook, maybe with the title "How to reorient my life." It is worth recording your notes in permanent form as the workshops will help you develop a plan tailored specifically to your needs. This plan will help you jump off the frenzied treadmill and steer a course for your lighthouse. And for this we wish you every success!

Seven questions on how you see yourself

First of all, we would like to invite you to take a little test on the subject of life planning. Below are a number of statements. Please decide whether you think these statements are true or false and tick the relevant box.

Test: Seven statements – what do you think?

1. "Life cannot be planned – everything turns out differently to the way you expect."
   ☐ True   ☐ False

2. "My current projects are too important for me to bother with life planning."
   ☐ True   ☐ False

3. "I have a detailed daily plan that helps me structure my life."
   ☐ True   ☐ False

4. "Regular holidays are all I need in order to recharge my batteries and stay on top of things."
   ☐ True   ☐ False

5. "A good education guarantees that I'll be able to get ahead."
   ☐ True   ☐ False

6. "I know a lot about time and life planning and have my life under control."
   ☐ True   ☐ False

7. "I've mastered a whole raft of working techniques. That's how I organize my life."
   ☐ True   ☐ False

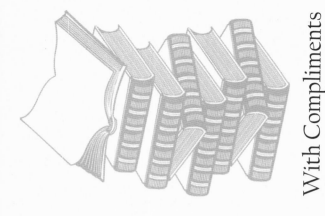

With Compliments

Hay-on-Wye Booksellers

13/14 High Town
Hay-on-Wye
Hereford
HR3 5AE

 01497 820352 / 875

www.hayonwyebooksellers.com

sales@hayonwyebooksellers.com

Answers

How many times did you tick "True"? You may be surprised to learn that ideally you should have answered "False" in each case. All the questions have been formulated in such a way that "False" is the correct answer each time.

Read the following explanation to find out why.

Misconception 1: "Life cannot be planned – everything turns out differently to the way you expect."

Planning is essential to our existence. Only by planning do we notice when we have drifted off course.

A little while ago we had a trainee at work who surprised us in the middle of the week by announcing that she had to finish work that very day even though she was not going on holiday until the weekend. It turned out that she still had a lot of things to sort out. Her ferry crossing had to be organized, the hole in her airbed mended and so on. She had a precise plan that she implemented in full over the next two or three days. When I asked whether she planned her everyday life as well as this, my question met with a look of incomprehension. "You can't plan your life!", she answered.

This is a commonly expressed view, but one that blatantly contradicts the old saying: *Only a fool does not make plans!* Those who plan do not claim that absolutely everything will work out as expected. In fact much happens differently, and yet it still makes very good sense to plan.

Planning has been described as the "management of variance." If you don't have a plan, of course, there can be no question of variance in the first place. An example will make this clear. A traveler is waiting on the platform – in vain – for his train. Eventually he goes up to the stationmaster and asks: "What's the point in having a timetable if my train is going to be 20 minutes late?" The stationmaster answers calmly: "If there were no timetable, Sir, how would you know your train was late?"

A misconception about planning is that it is always geared towards a minutely detailed, long-term prescription for the future, but this is only true in certain cases. There are many different forms and levels of planning. A more detailed form of planning is called for, for example, if you are putting together your schedule for tomorrow or if your task is to draw up the timetable for a Mars landing in 2015. However, the longer your perspective, the more approximate your planning will be. In this long-term context, planning above all means "giving your life direction." It is fascinating to study the lives of the famous and successful. Almost all of them had a goal in mind that they wanted to achieve above all else: a career, an invention, a task, a building...

What is your goal? Where do you want to be in three, five or fifteen years' time? Where do you want to be by the end of your life? What kind of stamp do you want to put on your life? What do you want to have achieved? Can you sense what an enormous influence the answers to these questions will have on your life? What we are talking about here is the art of *having the end in sight at the beginning*. This art will make an important contribution to your quality of life. We are talking about sensible, far-sighted behavior. If this can become a way of life, it will save a great deal of unnecessary pain and suffering.

Admittedly it is not easy to give your own life direction. But if you don't do it yourself, you are leaving it up to your mother-in-law, your boss, your partner, your children. Is this what you want? It is *your* life. Life is something that is incredibly precious – let's look after it as though we only have one.

During the course of our counseling work, we have met hundreds of people who have only ever been the object of other people's desires and expectations. At some point, though, enough is enough! There was a 75-year-old woman who expressed her regret in one of our seminars that she had only ever done what her husband and those around her had expected of her. Following the death of her husband, she finally wanted to discover her life. If she were to live as long as her mother had lived, she would still have 15 valuable years left and she wanted to decide for herself, for once, how to live them. A wise decision indeed! But why wait until you're 75?

If you are facing the challenge of drawing up a concrete plan for your life for the first time, you are bound to be wondering: how do I go about this? At school and at home, it is unusual for us to be focused enough to devise a life plan extending decades into the future. Perhaps you will be frightened at the prospect of breaking out of the familiar and doing something new with your life. But it is a worthwhile goal! Seneca got to the heart of the matter when he wrote: "If I know not what harbor I seek, then no wind is the right wind." What this means for us is that once we know where we want to go with our lives, we can direct all our strength and resources into moving in the right direction.

Give your life direction! Become the principal shareholder in your own life!

Misconception 2: "My current projects are too important for me to bother with life planning."

Your most important project is your life! It is the only project whose outcome is ultimately decisive for you.

Have you ever visited a film set? You see a lot of wonderful scenery that makes you feel you are in a beautiful city, but if you take time to stop and go through one of the decorative doors, you are brought quickly down to earth. The illusion is held in place by a wooden framework. Behind the façade, you come face to face with reality. Is your apparently successful life a mere façade masking a lack of planning or purpose?

We naturally assume that most of what we do is important. Once we are in the hamster wheel, however, it is often difficult to distinguish between things that are really important and those that only seem important. If the wheel is spinning too quickly, there is no time for reflection anyway.

It is worth considering the essential difference between the descriptions "important" and "urgent." Is it something that will bring you closer to your goal? If so, it is important. Or is it merely urgent? If it is urgent it requires your immediate attention, but achieving it won't actually take you any further forward. What we describe as important is generally only urgent. Going to the dentist once a year is important. If you happen to get toothache, a visit to the dentist becomes a matter of urgency. For a number of decades we have been making the observation – which many people find surprising – that what is important is seldom urgent and what is urgent is seldom important. This is examined in more detail in a later chapter: "Implement Offensively" (see pages 157–212).

In order to be able to differentiate between the things that are truly important and those that are only apparently important in our lives, we have to take time out on a regular basis. We need time to pause, get off the wheel, look behind the scenery of our own lives and consider what will provide us with a solid foundation on which to build a life – and discover what is mere illusion.

Another (old and rediscovered) word for this time of reflection is contemplation. This involves stopping to consider whether the meaning you ascribe to a particular matter is real or simply a mirage. In examining their own lives, many people have stopped seeing the connection between today and tomorrow. What will really get me ahead and what is mere action for the sake of action? Of course, in order to be able to judge what will get me ahead I need to ask: where do I want to get to? The answer to this question can be crucial to your psychological well-being. This point was made by poet William Blake: "He who desires but acts not, breeds pestilence."

Among the chief enemies of our deliberately planning and organizing our lives are our own busy, active natures. You may know the scene in the film *Titanic* in which a man on the sinking ship pauses in his escape to reset a clock that is showing the wrong time. While his action is "correct" and conscientious, it is also completely futile.

So, despite the demands of all your important or not so important projects, make sure you regularly take a sensible amount of time to escape the "urgency trap."

Misconception 3: "I have a detailed daily plan that helps me structure my life."

Daily planning is a view from below, a mole's perspective, so to speak. What you need is an eagle's perspective; you need to gain an overview of the whole picture.

A good daily plan is an indispensable work tool that gives us control over our daily tasks. Personal organizers have established themselves as an irreplaceable tool in our lives. If you plan only on a daily basis, however, you run the risk of simply reacting to events. It is easy to lose the overview that is absolutely necessary in order to take sensible long-term decisions.

Good day-to-day planning will help you structure your day. Good life planning will help you steer your life in the right direction!

At some time or other, you must have had the opportunity to enjoy the view from a mountain summit. You can trace the path you took up the mountain. And on the other side lies the route along which you want to continue. In the far distance you can see your destination: the highest, most beautiful peak for miles around. The path that leads to it is partly hidden in valleys and ravines, behind mountaintops and beneath clouds. The picture becomes imprinted on your inner, emotional map and you know you are going in the right direction! Despite the ups and downs, it is the most sensible route. Even if it is often concealed, your destination exists and you will get there if you continue along the route.

Which is more important: simply to press forward or regularly to take the time you need to get your bearings? In order to reach your destination, you need to do both! Don't fool yourself where life expectancy is concerned. Life insurers' mortality charts are blunt: women can expect to live to a good 80 and men to 74. Compared with earlier generations, these are great ages. On the other hand, life is hardly an eternity. However, many people live their lives as if death were something that only happens to other people. Don't forget that the death rate for *Homo sapiens* is and always has been 100 percent. Death catches everybody, even if we try not to think about it. It is therefore extremely sensible to get an overview of our own lives and to slot the present into the appropriate place.

This book invites you to take a metaphorical trip in a helicopter, to examine your life from an eagle's perspective. There is your

workplace, over there is your home, your marriage, your children's school... You will see beautiful-looking areas that make your heart beat faster – as well as areas whose existence you would rather deny. You will discover building sites, structures that are at risk of collapsing and underdeveloped areas; regions that have not been watered for a long time, but also gardens full of flowers.

At some point you will have to land. That is when you'll start clearing up, planting trees and shoring up structurally weak areas. Your eagle's perspective will have helped you to see your life in a new and different light. You will have a new, realistic overview and will be able to start collecting, sorting and assessing again. This will prevent you wasting time on the unimportant areas of life.

Don't take refuge in doing things for the sake of doing them without first gaining an overview. The price you have to pay for this is higher than you think! We all plan for the day ahead, sometimes for the month ahead, but rarely for the whole year ahead. Longer stretches of time, such as a seven-year period or a

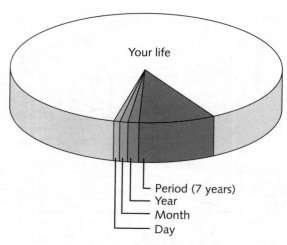

The available time in your life

lifetime, are excluded from this planning process altogether. Those who do have an eye on their whole lives, however, do not get tangled up in the undergrowth of daily tasks.

Misconception 4: "Regular holidays are all I need in order to recharge my batteries and stay on top of things."

Of course you need physical recuperation. But holidays alone do not solve the problem of finding meaning in life. Only those who understand the meaning of their actions can feel truly secure. Even a year-long holiday would not deal with the issues of vision, values and meaning.

People become depressed, unwell and lose all sense of enthusiasm as a result of no longer being able to see any meaning in their lives, in their destiny. According to a study conducted by the medical insurance companies and employers' liability insurance associations, stress-related illnesses are most common in cases where individuals perceive their jobs and lives as meaningless. When the value of what these individuals do is revealed to them, they become healthy again. No doubt many of this book's readers will have had the experience of finding a task far easier to perform when it seems meaningful.

The question of personal happiness in our private lives is also closely bound up with the question of meaning. This was discovered by renowned American happiness researcher Mihaly Csikszentmihalyi. Only by finding an answer to the question of meaning is it possible for us to "transform our whole lives into a unified flow experience," he writes in his bestseller *Flow: The Psychology of Happiness* (p. 281). Meaning is thus an important motivating factor. Meaninglessness, on the other hand, is a devourer of energy. It robs us of our sleep, our "good conscience" and our effectiveness.

Misconception 5: "A good education guarantees that I'll be able to get ahead."

A good education may form the basis for almost any career, but it is nowhere near enough by itself. Precise, written planning is also needed.

A long-term study conducted at Harvard University into the professional careers of college-leavers leaves no doubt about the importance of written planning:

- 83 percent had no career aim. They were earning a certain average dollar amount.
- 14 percent had clear career aims, but these were not set out in writing. On average, they earned three times the amount earned by those with no career aims.
- 3 percent had clear career aims that they had put in writing. On average they were earning ten times as much as those with no aims.

Naturally, a good education is worth its weight in gold and offers a solid basis for a career. But how do you build on this basis? Never in the history of mankind has the amount of knowledge available worldwide increased as quickly as it is increasing today. Between 1800 and 1900, the amount of information available doubled, and it doubled again in 1950, 1970 and 1980. At the current time, the amount of knowledge available worldwide is doubling at least every four years. In certain areas, such as information technology, the rate of increase is considerably higher still. This has enormous consequences on our lives and professional development. Change is occurring significantly faster than ever before!

To keep up to date, we have to continue our education and training. Confronted by the torrent of information flowing continually in our direction, we each have to establish our own foci. The days of one-off education are past: lifelong learning is now the name of the game. It is no longer the education secretary or the syllabus that is in charge of your education – it is you yourself! Responsibility rests with you, which is why education and training also belongs in your (written) life plan.

Researchers assume that those currently under 30 years old will pursue between four and six different professions during their lifetime. Different *professions*, not different positions! Technological and social changes render old professions superfluous and give rise to new ones. And often the tools used change radically within the same profession. Just think about typesetters, who may initially have learned hot-metal setting but are required today to be computer experts.

Things change. Who is responsible for your personal reaction to this change? Your boss, the politicians, society, your mother...? No, you are. Each of us has to be the entrepreneur of our own life. How often have you left it to someone else to tell you how to react to a particular situation? It's time to stop! Don't let someone else write your biography. If you don't know how to proceed with something, call in an adviser – that's quite in order and is often very important. But take the decision yourself. After all, it's your own life.

We have started to lose sight of the principle of taking responsibility for ourselves. Werner Then, former chairman of the German Association of Catholic Businessmen (the BKU) summed up the situation in Germany: "Personal responsibility is effectively outlawed in this country. Our lives are regulated by 70,000 laws and ordinances. The unions and employers want to dictate our every step. We even choose holidays whose every aspect is decided in advance. What we need is to return to a culture of personal responsibility."

Assume personal responsibility for your life and career. The old model of education followed by work followed by peaceful, paid retirement no longer applies. It has been replaced by a colorful mix of education, work, retraining, work, a period of rest and professional reorientation, work, unemployment, sabbatical, work, part-time working in advance of retirement... You can blame nobody but yourself if you fail to take control of your own life. Making the transition from the old to the new model is not easy, but it is perfectly possible. The earlier you begin, the easier it will be. We have come across many older people who have made the (not entirely pain-free) switch and have grown to greatly appreciate the new model. Once the new has been integrated into your life, you will begin to benefit. The "adventure of life" will begin all over again – you will have become the director of the adventure film that is your own life.

Training is work – but it is worth the effort! Become the entrepreneur of your own life. This covers more than just your professional life. You will know you have reached an important step when you stop casting nostalgic glances at the past. Don't mourn missed opportunities. Forget the self-tormenting question: "Where would I be today if only I had...?" This is unproductive. Yesterday is yesterday, tomorrow is tomorrow and today is the time to be decisive.

Above all, never fall into the trap of thinking it is too late to set a new, trailblazing course. We are inclined to underestimate the opportunities on offer to those even of advanced age. Winston Churchill was 76 when he was elected Prime Minister of Britain for a second time. Konrad Adenauer stood again for Chancellor of the Federal Republic of Germany aged 85. The writer Ernst Jünger was 90 when he wrote his first detective novel and Polish pianist Mieczyslaw Horszowski could not be dissuaded from making another recording – of works by Bach, Schumann and Chopin – aged 98. It is never too late to seize new opportunities.

During the course of our seminar and counseling work we have been struck by the enormous dynamism of written planning. This is demonstrated by the Harvard University study cited above. Putting something in writing encourages a more deliberate interaction with it. Our recommendation therefore is that life planning should be put in writing and revised regularly. Not everyone finds this easy, but it clearly plays a fundamental role in "Getting Ahead." The process through which we will take you in this book is a thoroughly tried and tested tool designed to help you do this.

Misconception 6: "I know a lot about time and life planning and have my life under control."

Most people don't know how to use their extensive knowledge.

The longest distances to be mastered in this world are the paths from the head to the heart and from knowledge into action. Yes, we've read a lot of books, sat through lectures, seen talk shows and attended seminars. But this alone does not mean that we can benefit from the positive consequences of correct action.

A man came along to one of our seminars and said he was the best husband, most caring father and best boss he could imagine. The only problem was that neither his family nor his colleagues were prepared to endorse this. Through subsequent discussion we were able to help this extremely busy and well-meaning gentleman discover that while he understood a great many things theoretically,

the gap between theory and practice was enormous. It is worth recalling the words of the Protestant social reformer Gustav Werner: "That which is not made deed has no value!" Everyone struggles to some extent putting into practice what they already know. We know what to do, but we don't do what we know. In order to achieve balanced lives, therefore, we need to go beyond traditional time planning.

Misconception 7: "I've mastered a whole raft of working techniques. That's how I organize my life."

It is not so much a question of doing things the right way (efficiency) as doing the right things (effectiveness).

The clock is crucial for most people. Things have to be done faster and faster and precisely on time. Behind this is the demand for efficiency, for doing things the right way. Many of us end up running round in circles; no working techniques and no clock can help here. Put the clock aside for a moment and pick up a different tool – the compass. The compass helps us to answer the far more exciting question of which is the right direction.

Writer Gotthold Ephraim Lessing put it like this: "The slowest person who does not lose sight of his goal will always make faster progress than the person who wanders around aimlessly." We need workable goals! Goals that promise more than a quick kick. Goals that are worthy of commitment, investment, passion and effort. How many men and women have scrambled ambitiously up the career ladder only to find that the ladder is leaning against the wrong wall?

The PRO formula

The preceding test has exposed a number of commonly held misconceptions. The results throw up further questions, however. What do you do with this new knowledge? What consequences will it have for your life and career planning? These same questions crop up repeatedly in our seminars. In dealing with them, we have observed three different types of people.

- *People who don't know themselves.* People in this category have never thought deeply about their potential. The gifts and talents that lie dormant within them often remain undiscovered. Sometimes they take up careers that don't match their gifts at all, and end up unhappy. You can't turn a nightingale into a hawk. Each of these wonderful birds has its merits. We recognize the great diversity of species in nature and the different potential of each one, but people also have unique abilities. Many of our contemporaries have not yet made this discovery, however, and spend their time stealing envious or frustrated glances at others instead of discovering and developing their own potential. There is an inspiring saying that goes: "Success follows on when we follow what is in ourselves." Those who are not in harmony with their own potential will not be able to experience success in any deeper sense.

- *People who don't know where they want to go in life.* These people can be unsure about things for a number of reasons. They may never have had a goal in life worth striving for and live each day as it comes. Or else a life crisis (possibly a midlife crisis) may have shattered what previously seemed unshakeable in their lives. When asked about their goals in life, people in this category shrug their shoulders.
- *People who know where they want to get to, but don't set out on the road that leads there.* These people are generally frustrated. They have a thousand excuses for not living what is actually the most important thing for them. They lack energy and initiative but also the ability to say no at the right time. These people are not in harmony with themselves because there is a yawning gap between what they have and what they want.

Each of these types can be helped out of their unsatisfactory situations by the PRO formula as already outlined.

Those who use the PRO formula to rethink and replan their lives and then implement their plan offensively and proactively can enjoy a self-determined future. In the closing chapter of this book we look at "reaping the harvest" – how you can enjoy the fruit of your work. Calmness is not a Utopia, it is an opportunity. And you are currently on the best possible road to achieving it.

The hamster wheel – exertion without progress

You arrive home tired, your eyelids are heavy. You promise yourself an early night at last. But being the active person you are, you rush round the supermarket, make a couple of phone calls, do a few household chores and then prepare for the important business meeting you've got the next morning. You sit down, work for another hour or two and then watch a "little" television in order to relax. You're entitled to some rest time, after all. And finally you get to bed a lot later than planned. The next morning your alarm goes off early as usual. And off you go again: you wash,

grab a quick breakfast, travel to work, turn up for your appointments...

Have you ever watched one of those lovable little rodents on its hamster wheel? If not, take the time to do so. It is fascinating to observe how much energy can be expended without ever leaving the spot. The hamster wheel has become a symbol of our times. And we have invested a lot in continually improving our own hamster wheel. We've lubricated the bearing so that the wheel turns more freely; we've increased the size of the wheel and the distance between the rungs so that we can run faster. But we have lost sight of the fact that none of this is progress because when we are in the hamster wheel we never actually move forwards!

Maybe you know the feeling that you've been rushing and running around all day but don't seem to have achieved anything. You meant to get ten things done, but you have only done two of them. Continual phone calls, visitors without appointments, faxes stamped "urgent," meetings that overrun... The mill has been clattering away all day long but has produced very little flour.

Geraldine, a "typical" mother and housewife, tells a similar story: "I've no time. In the morning I get up, wake the children, make breakfast and make sure they all leave the house neat and tidy and on time. That leaves just three hours to put the house in order before I collect the youngest child from playgroup. We have lunch and then the older children get home from school and want a snack. Every afternoon one or other of the children has to be taken to sports training or music lessons. Then it's homework time. My mother-in-law might have a birthday, in which case I have to get everything ready for Saturday and then there's the garden – oh dear, the garden... At ten o'clock I fall into bed tired out. I don't have any time for myself."

A good routine is healthy; on the other hand, incessant running around is unhealthy and leads to illness. Normally, stress is only a short-term condition and is not, therefore, harmful. It becomes dangerous when the feeling of stress becomes long term. According to a study conducted in Germany, at least 15 percent of German management staff suffer from a form of permanent stress and inability to relax. What are the consequences?

An article in the German journal *Psychologie heute* [Psychology Today] cites scientific studies confirming that intense and chronic stress *directly* weakens the immune system. This leads to health problems and has a detrimental effect on any pre-existing illnesses. In his article, psychoneuroimmunologist Dr. Ronald Glaser takes into account the findings of over 85 studies. The good news is that behavioral therapy techniques can bring about significant improvements even to the immune system – another good reason for reading this book to the end.

Life in the hamster wheel affects more than just our bodies, however. Our creativity also suffers enormously from the effects of unhealthy, long-term stress. Have you ever had good new ideas during periods of persistent stress? A lot of creativity is lost when

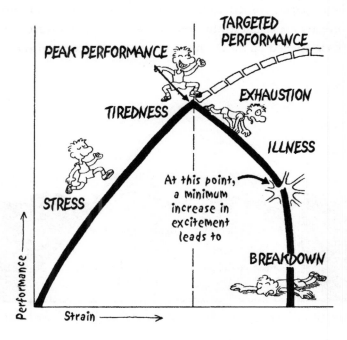

we can do nothing but pant away in the hamster wheel and our only goal is to survive the day.

Do you live or are you lived? Do you shape your life or are you being shaped? Is it actually possible to achieve a healthy balance in our lives between calm and excitement? Life is hard work. Are calm and talk of a self-determined future merely a dream, a populist promise made by the self-appointed high priests of motivation? Are there any principles that hold true for everyone? We would like to issue a warning at this point: beware of models that might work for X, Y or Z, but don't work for you. Not everything is transferable. The real question is: how do I build a healthy, fulfilled life that is tailored to my own needs? How do I succeed in determining my own future? These are questions you can't answer by following set patterns, but only by taking into account your individual personality.

The following pages have been written with the aim of taking you on a journey of discovery. Many of our seminar participants have already experienced this journey as a "voyage towards calm," which has opened up for them the way to a self-determined future.

Our time planning is merely the visible tip of our hidden inner world

What motivates you?

We are motivated to act by two main factors: pain and pleasure. Our efforts to avoid the first and enjoy the second are stronger than any other driving impulses.

In principle, these two factors operate in all men and women. If we look at the model that lies at the heart of advertising, we will find these exact promises: those who buy product X will experience no more pain in a particular area of life, but instead will enjoy extremely pleasant feelings. Think of a toothpaste advert, for example, which promises the avoidance of painful tooth decay and dental work and the pleasure of having healthy white teeth and increased confidence and social success.

If our pain in a particular matter is great enough, we will suddenly be prepared to take on things that would previously have struck us as "far too taxing" and unpleasurable. There are numerous examples of this. Harry was a dynamic manager in his early forties. He had published several books, was head of a large organization, and traveled a great deal giving lectures and seminars and advising people. The feedback from his work was overwhelmingly positive. People reported back gratefully on the fantastic, helpful counseling they received thanks to his commitment. At home he was a good father to a large family. One day, he had a heart attack out of the blue that told him: you're doing too much! During an interesting recovery period he learned not to accept every invitation. He learned to say no, to listen to his body and to introduce a healthy dose of physical exercise into his life. Unfortunately he had rarely found time for this before...

Another successful businessman built up a number of profitable companies, crossed the Atlantic in Concorde, was a passionate pilot and did a lot of good deeds with his wealth. He had just two weaknesses: overeating and avoiding exercise. These weaknesses cost him his life at just 53.

In response to a wide range of alarm signals, many of us realize: "You can't go on like this!" Our relationship with our partner may be very strained or we may be reduced to "living side by side with them in the same house." We may have hardly any contact with the children any more. Our mountain of debt may be growing dramatically. We may weigh 20 pounds more than we did two years ago. Our best workers may be continually leaving the firm. We may not have any friends left. At work we may be simply reacting, complaining about unreliable people and lousy business conditions. Of course we all know that there is no life without hard work and pain. Much of the misery, however, is of our own making or is unnecessary and avoidable if we pay heed to the alarm signals and take the necessary action.

One of our time management seminars took place in a heart clinic in a beautiful setting. This venue was recommended to us because of its pleasant seminar rooms. While we were discussing the consequences of long-term stress on people's health, on the terrace on the other side of the window we could see a number of patients – men of our own age – who apparently had a lot of time on their hands. During the break some of these patients asked us what kind of seminar we were conducting. When they were told it was on "time management for executives", they told us that among them were "senior managers," a "leading figure in the automobile industry" and so on. Of course, it was their lifestyles that caused them to end up here. In response to our queries about what the patients were planning to do differently, the group immediately began to brag about who had had the most bypasses. Clearly no deep reflection had set in. The seminar participants watched in silence and shook their heads gently. A senior manager thanked us after the event – it couldn't have made more of an impression on him.

Of course, we can wait until our own pain is sufficiently great for the necessary willingness to make changes to kick in. In our counseling we have repeatedly encountered people who possessed no more than a small readiness to change, who hoped that the counselor would produce some kind of magic potion that would enable them to achieve positive change in their lives without their putting in any effort. These people are mistaken. Change is only possible if you *want* to change. Some people want to change out of sheer good sense, others as a result of their own damaging and painful experiences. For the sake of your nerves, we recommend that you embrace change for the first reason.

What does changing mean? Up to now, you have done things a certain way. Experience has shown you, however, that the way you are doing things is destructive. It is robbing you of your quality of life and affecting your work and relationships. You are living with the continual feeling that you are missing your goals and failing to get where you want to be. You therefore decide to adopt a new and better form of behavior. To combat old habits is extremely hard work, however.

People automatically get older, but they do not necessarily become more mature. Becoming more mature means learning from the "avoidable" pain we have experienced and switching to a different type of behavior.

Many experiences can be acquired more cheaply second hand. Pain and pleasure, our main motivating driving forces, can manifest themselves as incentives in the form of real-life models. Imagine one of your colleagues achieves remarkable results using a particular method. Are you not also motivated (even in secret) to try to use the same method? Usually, this process occurs unconsciously.

Wisdom means pausing for a moment in cases like this – not immediately reacting, but thinking, weighing things up and adopting a workable course of action. Seeing what my colleague has achieved spurs me on. But my colleague is my colleague, not me. What would suit me? What would be right for me? I don't want to copy what others are doing for the sake of it, I want to work out what is so fascinating about their thinking, talking and behavior that makes me want to emulate them.

Controlled or in control?

What prevents people from positively and creatively shaping their own lives? American academics examined this question in a study and made an interesting discovery. Most people tend to slip almost automatically into one of three destructive roles.

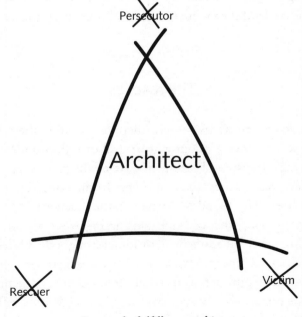

From role-fulfiller to architect

The victim

The first and possibly most obvious role that inhibits proactive, independent behavior is that of the victim. Do you know anyone who has slipped into this bad habit? Everyone but themselves is responsible for their plight: the politicians, their children, their partner, the boss, their work colleagues, the weather... Who will console the victim of this contemptible, evil world?

As a rule of thumb, only 10 percent of our lives cannot be changed; the remaining 90 percent can be directly influenced by our actions and reactions. Victims, on the other hand, always feel themselves to be the helpless objects of other people's actions. They are characterized by self-pity, moaning and passivity. From the first of these they draw their strength to live. This may feel like motivation, but it is an illusion, for it leads to the situation in which everything revolves exclusively around themselves and their own cares. The *credo* of the victim is: I am nothing but a poor wretch.

The rescuer

Rescuers love victims. Wherever there are victims there is some rescuing to be done. Without a great deal of reflection, feelings of sympathy are transposed into action. It might seem very noble to be a rescuer, but rescuers prevent others from taking responsibility for their lives. The Good Samaritan in the rescuer reacts to need and displays sympathy without considering what would actually be right for either the immediate or long term good. While victims draw their vital energy from self-pity, rescuers are generally characterized by pure activism. What often seems very helpful from the outside can also be a way of avoiding having to stop, reflect and look for the right solution.

Can you think of people you know who often prefer to act straightaway rather than pause to think and weigh up what the right course of action would be in that particular situation?

The persecutor

Where there are rescuers and victims, the third member of the trinity, the persecutor, will not be far away. Persecutors always shift responsibility onto others. Unlike victims, who wallow in self-pity, the *modus operandi* of followers is to attack! They complain, get angry and polemicize. Do you know people who can never be blamed for anything? It's always other people who are responsible for the failure of a project... If only other people weren't so lousy, everything would be just fine.

Workshop: My favorite role

Each of the three roles is present to some degree in all of us. Nevertheless, everyone has his or her favorite role. Which is yours? Which is your secondary role? Perhaps you play a different role in each area of your life?

The following questionnaire is designed to help you discover which role is the main obstacle that prevents you from proactively shaping your life. Please indicate to what extent each of the following statements applies to you. Don't answer according to how you would like to be, but according to how you actually behave. Perhaps you could ask a friend or your partner to evaluate you?

Statement	applies 1	applies to a large extent 2	applies to some extent 3	applies to a lesser extent 4	hardly applies at all 5	does not apply 6
When I am under stress...						
1. I knuckle down and become active.						
2. I hold back and ask myself what this situation means for me.						
3. I get annoyed with others for their share of the blame for my stress.						
When I come under attack from others during the course of a conflict...						
4. I prefer to keep my mouth shut and try to remain calm and quiet. It's not usually worth saying anything anyway.						
5. I confront the other person.						
6. I become active and do what I can to remove the cause.						
Other people often cause...						
7. me to feel good.						
8. me to feel bad.						
9. others to feel good.						
10. others to feel bad.						
In general, it is important that I...						
11. defend myself, otherwise other people will take advantage of me at some point.						
12. support others because this automatically brings about an improvement in the long term.						

Please enter your scores in the relevant box:

	No.	Rescuer	No.	Persecutor	No.	Victim
	1		3		2	
	6		5		4	
	9		10		7	
	12		11		8	
Total						

Your favorite role is the role with the lowest score. Please also consider the context you had in mind when answering the questions. Do you assume the same role in both your professional and private life?

A lot of people have the astonishing ability to switch from one role to another within a matter of seconds. From this role we draw strength, a sense of direction and orientation. Rescuers, for example, run the risk of drawing their self-affirmation and identity exclusively from their role as helpers, and the same is true for the other roles. Each of these roles is destructive and prevents us from carrying out the real task of consciously shaping our lives! Charles Swindoll got to the heart of it in the following:

The longer I live, the more I realize the impact of attitude on life.
Attitude, to me, is more important than facts.
It is more important than the past, than education, than money, than circumstances, than failures, than successes, than what other people think or say or do.
It is more important than appearance, giftedness or skill.

It will make or break a company... a church... a home.
The remarkable thing is we have a choice every day regarding the attitude we will embrace for that day.
We cannot change our past... we cannot change the fact that people will act in a certain way.
The only thing we can do is play on the one string we have, and that is our attitude...

I am convinced that life is 10 percent what happens to me and 90 percent how I react to it.

And so it is with you... we are in charge of our attitudes.

There may be 10 percent of our lives that we cannot shape, but still this leaves 90 percent that we can! Even if 20 percent of your life could not be changed, that would still leave 80 percent that can be. (If your instinct tells you that the percentage of your life that you can change is lower, this could be due to an unusual, temporary state of affairs although the reason is more likely to be that you are a "victim.")

Become the architect of your life, your future. Discover the many opportunities not just to react to things, but to shape them.

> It's all in your state of mind
>
> If you think you are beaten, you are.
>
> If you think you dare not, you don't.
>
> If you like to win but think you can't
> It is almost certain you won't.
>
> If you think you'll lose, you're lost.
>
> For out of the world we find
> Success begins with a fellow's will.
>
> It's all in your state of mind.
>
> (Anonymous)

Don't be afraid of life's new phases

Human life has been ingeniously designed. Our lives are structured in such a way that we pass through numerous different phases. Each phase includes its own development task. Only by coping successfully with this development task are we able to mature. You know the different phases: development in the womb – childhood – young adulthood and so on.

Something is missing in this description of life's different periods, however: the transitional stages between phases. People going through a transitional stage usually perceive their situation as a crisis. Our time in the womb – the bathtub-like warmth, the muted light, the agreeable rhythm of our mother's heartbeat, the voices of other family members growing ever more familiar – is abruptly interrupted by external pressure. The baby is squeezed through a small opening into the outside world. This world, which is cold, frightfully bright and loud – we even have to work in order to get our nourishment... Psychologists say birth is the greatest crisis of our lives. Congratulations! All of you reading this book have already mastered the most difficult crisis of all.

The phase of childhood is a highly formative time. Not only do we learn to walk, read and write, we also learn how to handle other people. We learn to confront issues and how to bring them to a conclusion. We learn to learn. The foundations are laid for our whole conception of self, the world and our fellow human beings. Then comes the well-known crisis (or transitional stage) of puberty. During this period we are neither children nor adults, we want to be both at the same time and yet we want to be neither. This is not an easy time for teenagers and those around them – as you no doubt know from your own experience...

Eventually we make the leap into adulthood. Youthful vigor is the name of the game. We live our new freedom to the full, coming home when we want to, acquiring our own flats and cars, making our own decisions.

All of a sudden we find ourselves facing a new transition, which Romano Guardini calls the Ideal-Real Crisis. We want to create the largest software company in the world, carry on demonstrating until the whole planet becomes a nuclear-free zone, spend our whole life visiting foreign countries – but then we come up against the limits of reality. Not that our basic preoccupations are necessarily wrong, it is just that our idealism finds itself confronting the real world face-to-face.

The years dominated by getting established, working and building up our lives are then followed by a midlife crisis. We have passed 40, our physical strength is no longer what it was, our priorities change. If we work alongside younger adults we notice a difference. We fall into bed exhausted at 11 o'clock after a long day at work whereas our younger colleagues will be meeting their friends at the café or bar and discussing what to do next.

One of the typical questions we ask during the midlife crisis is: do I want to do what I am doing for the rest of my life? Whereas the first half of one's life is characterized by a striving for success, the focus of the second half of our lives gradually moves towards giving our lives meaning.

In order to ensure that the individuals concerned had mastered their earlier crises, the ancient Greeks only allowed those aged over 50 to play an active role in politics. This is a phase in which we can work extremely effectively due to our experience of life. In a performance comparison between experienced older workers (50+) working normally and college-leavers slogging away at a 50- to 60-hour week, it was found that the older generation achieved more effective results in a significantly shorter space of time. This observation stands in contradiction to the current bias towards youth in the business world – especially where recruitment is concerned. Younger employees may on average spend less time off sick, but more time spent at the workplace does not make up for decades of professional experience.

The next life crisis occurs around the age of 65. Here the object is to let go and pass on the fruits of our life's work to others. It is all about discovering the opportunities inherent in the aging process and not giving up out of fear or comfort or clinging desperately to everything one has achieved in the past. Former senior managers in this age group often get together to mentor young entrepreneurs – to help them out with advice and offer active support too. This is a wonderful opportunity to achieve great things free from operational duties and usually free from financial pressures as well. Many well-known figures have achieved a "third" body of work during this phase. One example is Dutch woman Corrie Ten Boom, who

in her seventies started making films about her life under the
Nazi regime.

In old age we also have plenty of time to concentrate on our
relationships once more. Many senior managers describe how their
grandparents exerted a formative influence on their lives. Enriched
by the influence of your thinking and values, perhaps your
granddaughter could become a great leader of her country! It goes
without saying that even if she does not make it to the top, this is
still a valuable investment of your time! Old age is an important
phase during which we can make an active contribution to society
as advisers, independent thinkers and co-shapers.

Discover opportunity in crisis

The Chinese have no individual character for *crisis*. The character they use is made up of two different symbols, the one for *chance* and the other for *problem*.

Whatever the reason for the crisis, the situation of the person undergoing it will always incorporate both aspects. The crises of development described above are inevitable, though they may take

The Chinese character for **crisis**

The Chinese character for **problem**　　The Chinese character for **chance**

Crisis – Problem – Chance

a variety of forms. They are part of the development process for people who want to mature.

We need to be absolutely clear about one thing: there is no short cut. Without these elemental crises we cannot mature and our personalities will remain underdeveloped. A caterpillar spins a cocoon around itself and after its metamorphosis into a butterfly it must then undergo the strength-sapping process of breaking out of this husk. If we help the butterfly hatch out of its cocoon, we are doing it a disservice. It is precisely this exertion that gives the insect its ability to fly. This "crisis" alone allows it to develop what is necessary for flight. A butterfly that is removed from its cocoon by a third party will not be able to climb up into the air. It will fall to the ground and perish.

People and their situations change. Things that were applicable and right and worked wonderfully during one life phase suddenly cease to be workable. Our task is to find a personal, constructive response to each new situation. Whatever the reason for your crisis, while it is always a challenge and a risk, it is an opportunity too.

"Hallelujah!"

It may initially seem like a threat, but it is also an opportunity to discover new things, to further our development, to mature and to assume responsibility for a new situation in life. Hence the profound saying: when God wants to give you a gift, he wraps it up in a problem.

Remarkably, two-thirds of all prizewinning companies come from the same sector. You probably think this is going to be the service sector or the high-tech industries. Wrong! It is actually automobile manufacturers and their suppliers. Nowhere is competition fiercer than in the car industry. Suppliers are regularly confronted with the need to cut prices. Those who do not go along with this are replaced by others. Crises of this sort lead to change and consequently, in many cases, to peak performance.

Crises are an exciting time and a great opportunity to escape well-worn patterns of behavior and improve. We can seize the opportunity, push it away or rebel against it. Perhaps you know people who are biologically 50 years old, but have never really stopped being teenagers? A lot of people fight desperately (and unsuccessfully) against growing old. But each stage of life has its attractions and is beautiful in its own way. It is of great benefit to society if the different generations, each with their own strengths and weaknesses, can enrich each other's lives through a conscious desire to co-exist.

We should also see the transition into retirement in this light – not as the dumping of our own lives on some parking lot, but as the passage into a phase of new challenges. Amazing things have been achieved by people over 65 years of age! The opinion pollster Elisabeth Noelle-Neumann, herself an astonishing example of fruitful activity in old age, said in an interview: "So tell old people they will only be happy by remaining as active as possible. For example, by helping the younger generation without demanding thanks. Help the young people even if they are ungrateful, for that is not the issue. The important thing is that I can see that I have helped my children." In the context of her research, Mrs. Noelle-Neumann has repeatedly pointed out that rising to new challenges gives a person new strength and is a source of happiness. This is true for each of life's phases!

Crises that are pushed away rather than being dealt with are not solved; at best they lie dormant. At the first opportunity, this unfinished business will come back to haunt you. And this time around it is usually more difficult to deal with as you may have the next crisis on your hands at the same time.

Become more mature, not just older! People who mature in character as they advance in years experience an enormous increase in their quality and enjoyment of life as they grow older. Those who refuse to do this are engaging in a futile battle to maintain an illusion that ultimately fools no one. Do you know the fairy tale *The Emperor's New Clothes*? In it a clever tailor attempts to outwit a king and his people. For a large sum of money he agrees to provide the Emperor with a new suit of clothes, but merely pretends to dress him, not actually giving him any new garments to wear. His trick was to say that only the stupid could not see the fine cloth he was using. Frightened of making fools of themselves, the Emperor and his subjects praise the new suit of clothes. The swindle is only exposed when a child dares to call out: "But he's not wearing any clothes!"

In each of these crises we are confronted by a number of typical questions formulated in a variety of different ways: What have I actually been doing for all these years? Who am I? What am I capable of? What will I do over the coming years? How will I live my life? How can I implement my plans? In order to emerge from these crises as more mature individuals, it is essential that we do not shirk these questions. The key to a better future lies in finding workable answers to them.

First step:
Discover your potential

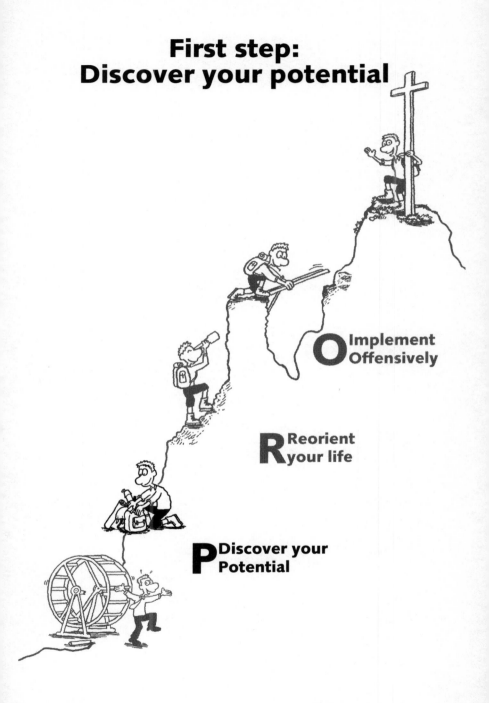

"Everyone is born an original, but many die as copies."

Anonymous

One demonstration of the genius of all creation is the so-called pear tree principle. We can recognize the leaf of a pear tree anywhere in the world from its structure – and yet each pear leaf on the planet is unique. The same is true for you: you too are unique! Over the following pages we will provide you with a tool that will enable you to understand yourself and others better and, as a result, to actively shape your life. You will notice that despite the fact that we are using a grid, there are still limitless opportunities to do justice to your inspired uniqueness, for whatever you may have in common with others, you are still unique.

The differences between our natures, talents and potential are also closely associated with our opportunities to do or not to do certain things. My five-year-old nephew surprised me after having a leg amputated, as a result of cancer, with the sober observation that he probably wouldn't be able to play football for Bayern Munich now. The youngster is therefore on the look-out for an alternative possible career.

What is my potential? What am I capable of? Who am I? What drives me? What fascinates me? What is it that makes my life worth living? According to the latest scientific studies, some factors would appear to be an inherent part of us, to be innate. Others stem from our upbringing, the environment in which we grew up, our life story. Still others take shape and develop throughout our whole life and are themselves subject to change.

This chapter focuses on the treasure hunt for your potential. You will discover how fascinating it is to find out more about yourself. All of a sudden you will understand why one thing or another is important to you and is part of who you are. At the same time an awareness will develop of the differences between people and thus of their uniqueness. Our potential is not, however, something fatalistic which leaves only one route open to us. It is a kind of foundation on which we can build. The closer we scrutinize this foundation, the more solid our basis for the future. What you then do with it is up to you. You will see that once you have become familiar with this foundation, you will discover more opportunities for subsequent building than you would have expected.

Admittedly a certain amount of work lies ahead. We have devised numerous workshops to help you uncover your potential. Everything has been made as simple as possible while remaining as differentiated as it inevitably needs to be. You are a complex individual with a rich life history and a wealth of gifts! You cannot therefore be fathomed out in a couple of trite checklists. What we would really like to do at this stage is give you a friendly slap on the back and say: don't lose heart! Embark upon this process because it will provide the key to a self-determined future. We know a lot of people who have taken this step and achieved a depth and intensity of life of which they could only previously have dreamed.

Do you have reservations about this process because your potential is changing and continuing to develop? This is precisely why it is important to take time out *regularly* (annually, for example) to reflect on your own life. Most importantly, this will teach you to think in a particular way. This way of thinking will gradually help you to become less and less the plaything of external circumstances and, building on your potential, talents and inclinations, will help you reflect upon and shape your life in a responsible way.

Regular time out: the dream day

"I'll think it over by myself" – a frequently used expression and a good idea, especially when what you need to think about is something as important as your life. The process of reflecting, finding answers and making good decisions cannot lead to workable results in the longer term if it is carried out amid the hectic rush of everyday life. Those who want to shape their lives need at least short periods of "time out."

This is precisely why a new and very sensible trend has developed for "dream days" of all kinds. Many use the more traditional terms "retreat" or "seclusion" to describe the same event. Indeed, the word "cloister" comes from the Latin word for an enclosed space away from the hustle and bustle of the world.

A number of executives regularly take time to withdraw, to clamber off the hamster wheel of everyday life. Their purpose is to reflect on the question: do I really want to do what I am doing? Am I living in harmony with my own needs, with the key areas of my life (partnership, family, finances, health…)? Does my high level of commitment actually make sense or is it merely an inability to relax – pure bustle, remotely controlled by the desires, expectations and needs of others?

You can escape the hamster wheel in one of the following ways:

- You can wait until the hamster wheel breaks down, either through wear and tear or due to an accident (heart attack, for example).
- You can climb off it!

Of course, there are also irresponsible ways of climbing off and there is also a certain risk of injury involved. But consider the lack of responsibility and the consequences of powering the hamster wheel relentlessly on and on with your own feet.

In a questionnaire, executives confirmed that their most creative ideas occur to them not during the prescribed work time in the office, but during long car journeys, in the bathtub, on the toilet, during a concert, in the sauna… Apparently their time at the office is so full of things that have to be seen to immediately and in person that hardly any time remains for creative work.

This has also been confirmed by Professor Dr. Birnbaumer, a brain research scientist at the University of Tübingen: "During the course of our investigations into the dynamics of the human brain during productive intellectual activity, we have been able to establish so to speak empirically that the likelihood of new and surprising ideas and insights occurring is at its greatest when we leave the brain in peace, protected as much as possible from the endless stream of external stimuli that constantly clamor for our attention. Today's world presents the opposite picture, its main feature apparently being the relentless flow of superfluous information."

It is precisely this insistent, superfluous information that we need to combat. We are subjected to an endless flow of such information, all of it proclaiming its special importance in whispers or shouts! The ringing telephone, the announcement of a TV special, e-mail messages, endless meetings with none but "important" people. Think about it: a lot of this is urgent, but for that very reason not necessarily really important. In the chapter entitled "Implement offensively" (see pages 157–212) we will give

you a number of useful tips on this subject. For now we would like to stress that as a rule you can only escape the urgency trap by making room for a sensible amount of time out and planning time. This will help ensure the quality of your professional and private life and ultimately even save you time. A dream day is not a holiday (although it may sometimes feel like it), but time taken for yourself on a regular basis in order to allow you to think about your life, your work and your career.

Whether it takes the form of a "quiet hour" in the office or a few days at a local retreat or in an isolated mountain lodge or attractive hotel, time out of this kind has a great deal in its favor. One of our seminar participants, a businessman, regularly visits a charming café with a view of the old center of his home town. Here he has an appointment with himself. He describes this monthly morning spent at his regular place in the café as the most important working time he has.

It is worth considering very carefully where you would best like to spend this time. Appropriate locations are places where there are not too many distractions, places that offer peace and quiet for thinking, places that inspire you. In the end, this time out is all about the fundamental orientation of your life. Do not on any account remain at home! The phone, your laundry, your family – maybe even your bed – will exert a powerful pull that will ruin your concentration. Don't go down to the cellar either! Most people find places that are located higher up more inspiring: a mountain lodge, a television tower restaurant, a vantage point of some kind. The feeling of overview will also affect the way you see your life. You will be able to see beyond the next day or the next few weeks. The dream day is a day on which you adopt an eagle's perspective and examine your life from above.

How you structure a dream day will depend very much on your own style. There are no rules as it is only the result that counts: that at the end of the day you know where your goals in life lie and know how to get your life back on course. Below is an *example* of what a dream day could look like. The individual elements mentioned here are explained in the following sections.

7.30	Walk to the shelter at the top of the mountain
8.00	Gain a sense of objectivity, make a note of things not yet done
8.30	Examine my own potential
9.30	Contemplate/visualize my goals in life and mission statement
	Describe/revise my defining visions
10.30	Redo workshops from the book *Where is your Lighthouse?*
11.30	For each of my roles in life (head of department, husband, chairman of social club etc.):
	– compare long-term goals and current commitment
	– establish interim goals for the coming months
14.00	Lunch in adjacent mountain restaurant followed by walk back

It can be useful to wrap a dream day up inside a recurring ritual. Once you have found an inspiring location, allow your dream day to follow the same pattern each time. Some people might spend the day in a café, opening their session by drinking a cappuccino and treating themselves to a slice of cake at the end of it. Others might feel happiest surrounded by a lot of bustle and spend the time between ten o'clock in the morning and three o'clock in the afternoon in a shopping mall. Still others might begin this time of thoughtfulness by reading an inspiring passage from the Bible and end their dream day with a prayer. Whatever the format, it should lead to the same end: to reset your life by your own compass and to make sure you don't neglect the things that are truly important to you.

In one of his books, Stephen Covey describes a group of forestry workers who saw wood industriously, without a break, in order to finish their work as quickly as possible. They are overtaken, however, by those who regularly pause and take time to sharpen their saws. We would like to recommend that you take at least two days' "time out" each year in order to "sharpen your saws." This book is ideally suited for use as the framework for orientation days of this type.

"To make it fair, everyone will undergo the same test:
you will all climb this tree!"

The next steps

Please remember: you are an original! It has been claimed that: "Everyone is born an original, but many die as copies." Let's make sure you do not go the same way! We have split the treasure hunt for our potential into the following steps:

What lies behind me?
- Understanding my history
- Discovering formative influences
- Overcoming obstacles in my life

What lies within me?
- Recognizing the abilities I enjoy using
- Understanding my personality structure
- Leading a valuable and value-filled life

In the next chapter our examination of your potential will look towards the future.

The story before your story

A question that is typically asked during times of crisis is: what have I been doing all these years? Have I been using my time well? Your past continually plays a decisive role when you come to examine the issue of your potential. Where did your story begin? In Central Europe, the answer to this normally starts something like this: "I was born on 17th May 1963 in Stuttgart…" In some cultures a quite different answer would be given to such a question: "I am the son of Charles and Diana Hinterhuber. My father is an engineer, my mother a housewife who worked as an architect until I was born." Do you notice the difference?

What came before

There is a Jewish family able to trace its family history back 2,000 years. Their forebears were Jewish writers who recorded the history of their people on papyrus scrolls. This history was passed down from generation to generation until the Middle Ages. During this period one of family's descendants worked with the inventor of letterpress printing, Johannes Gutenberg. He devoted his whole life to understanding every aspect of the printing technique. Another descendant, who had inherited the entire body of knowledge from his parents, later printed the first edition of the Book of Isaiah in northern Italy. The family remain writers and authors even to this day.

It is fascinating to see how knowledge and talent can be transmitted down through the centuries and continue to develop. This makes it all the more alarming that we so easily lose an awareness of our family and historical roots. The latest discoveries of genetic research demonstrate just how much genetic material we inherit from our parents. Fortunately it is not the case that everything is predetermined in detail, but our genetic origins nevertheless give us an essential stamp and a pool of characteristics on which we can build.

Imagine you are a master carpenter with your own carpentry shop. You have to take on a new trainee. There are two candidates. They are equally good in every respect and differ in just one way: one is the son of a carpenter while the other is the son of a butcher. Which of the two would you employ if you wanted to acquire a skilled co-worker as quickly as possible? The son of the carpenter,

naturally. From being a small child he has been able to see how the carpentry business works. He knows what it is all about; in all likelihood he will have started experimenting with wood as a youngster; he will be familiar with the smell of wood glue, will have applied paint to planed wood and will have watched his father doing a variety of different tasks. He will have learned to think like a carpenter and will know the world of carpentry better than the butcher's son.

All too often we forget the positive inheritance that is passed on to us by our parents. If your father was a skilled DIY enthusiast who knew how to handle all kinds of machinery, the chances are you will subconsciously have absorbed many of the same skills into your repertoire of talents. Whenever we had a party, my mother loved to decorate the whole flat. The main room was garlanded; the table was festively laid; flowers and candles played a prominent role. I notice today that when we have a celebration either at work or at home, I instinctively start to decorate the place. And can you guess what my children do? On Sundays and special occasions they decorate our dining table, jelly babies being their favorite item of decoration.

What characteristics have you inherited from your family? What did your father do for a living? What was your mother good at? Was she popular, a good actress in the local amateur dramatics society perhaps? Was she musical? Did she sing in the church choir? Did she enjoy company?

Many people find it easier to describe their parents' negative characteristics. Time and time again in our seminars, participants struggle with this workshop, for the question is not one they have considered. We would like to recommend a little trick that may help here. If you can think only of negative things, start by listing them on a separate piece of paper. Many negative characteristics are the flip side of positive qualities. For example, meanness can be an immature way of exercising thrift. Other similar pairs are garrulousness and affability, extravagance and generosity, thoughtlessness and courage, obstinacy and tenacity...

I was once giving a counseling session to a mechanical engineer. When we started to talk about this subject he opined that he was the first person who had inherited none of his parents' characteristics. This could be seen, he maintained, in the fact that his father was a farmer while he was a mechanical engineer with management responsibility. In reply to the question of how he came to enter his chosen profession, he declared that he had always loved tinkering with machines. Even as a teenager he used to take them apart and then put them together again. Where then, I wanted to know, did the considerable self-confidence come from that this demanded? He fell silent. After a while he said quietly: "From being a small child I used to watch my father take his tractor apart, clean it and reassemble it every year. He used to explain to me how important this was..."

It is not always easy to discover our own family inheritance. However well hidden, the astonishing thing is that the influence of our family is present nevertheless, in both positive and negative aspects. The popular saying has it that "The apple never falls far from the tree." What is your family inheritance, the story before your story?

Workshop: Family inheritance

In the following table, please write down the talents and abilities that exist or once existed in your family. What were your grandfather or grandmother particularly good at? What are your mother's or father's main characteristics?

	Special aptitudes, talents, distinctive personality traits etc.
Paternal grandfather	
Paternal grandmother	
Maternal grandfather	
Maternal grandmother	
Father	
Mother	
Uncle	
Aunt	
Brothers and sisters	

Examples

1. Aptitudes and talents
- music
- sports
- mathematics
- languages

2. Personality traits
- humorous
- extrovert
- intuitive
- loving
- eager to learn
- irritable

3. Appearance
- height
- eye and hair color
- build

4. Needs and wishes
- sleep
- preferences (e.g. food, colors, clothing)

5. Interests & hobbies
- reading
- animals/nature
- traveling
- going out
- gardening
- dancing

Which of these can I recognize in myself?

_____

_____

_____

My life story

Why are we asked for a résumé when applying for a job? A future employer wants to know what the applicant has learned, in which areas he has proved his worth, in which areas he has been given responsibility. Due to the variety of experiences and different areas of learning to which we are exposed, it is fascinating to draw up a comprehensive résumé of our lives. Assuming you have not spent the past years in a state of utter lethargy, you will have continually encountered new things. Of course, some things may need refreshing, such as training courses undertaken many years ago. Your résumé reveals where you have placed the emphasis in your life. Even if you want to do everything differently in future, it would be unwise to ignore the past.

Workshop: Taking stock

Whereas the previous analysis was more to do with looking objectively at your family background, this workshop asks subjective questions – how you would judge your family home, for example, or in what kind of company you feel at ease. Learn to get to know yourself better – perhaps you'll even give yourself a few surprises!

1. What was my earliest experience of success as a child that I can still remember clearly?

   _____

   _____

   _____

2. How would I view/judge my family home and upbringing?

   _____

   _____

   _____

3. What number child was I in the family and what effect did that position have on me?

   _____

   _____

   _____

4. Which of my parents was dominant and what influence did this have on my life?

   _____

   _____

   _____

What memories do I have of this in particular?

_____
_____
_____

5. What was my family like overall? Harmonious? Discordant? Was there a sense of cohesion?

_____
_____
_____

6. What influence did my home town and home region have on my life?

_____
_____
_____

What did I like about it? What bothered me about it?

_____
_____
_____

What were the reasons I left my home town (if applicable)?

_____
_____
_____

7. Which faith was I brought up in and what does that faith mean to me today?

_____
_____
_____

8. Which cultural factors have played a role in my life to date? How great is my interest in music and art?

_____

_____

_____

9. Which figures from the worlds of business, politics, culture, sport and other areas do I admire and why?

_____

_____

_____

What influence did or do these figures have on my development and decisions?

_____

_____

_____

You cannot and should not ignore the degree to which you have been shaped by your own past. There will have been highs and lows, things you can build on and things you are still struggling with today. During the course of your life you will have acquired important skills and amassed a wealth of experience. This is conveyed in your résumé. Have you ever looked at it from the point of view of your potential? It is astonishing how many different things you have learned during your life – from a foreign language, a musical instrument, texts relevant to your religion, all the way to flower arranging or using a circular saw at home. Some people will have learned book-keeping while others will have learned the basics of emotional intelligence at a weekend seminar. The list of things you have learned is probably longer than you think.

In the next workshop you will be changing your perspective. You will be examining your life from above, as it were, rather than looking at your development in the rear-view mirror.

Workshop: My development

On page 74 you will find a graduated scale, with numbers representing different ages. Above and below the horizontal line are indicators +6 and −6 to help you assess the way you felt when you were at a particular age. The assessment "−6" stands for "it was extremely difficult for me" and "+6" for "fantastic, it was a great time." Think about how you felt at certain times in your life and, using your assessments, draw a curve. Use the chart to ask yourself:

- How has my life gone so far?
- Where have the turning points been?
- In which direction am I currently moving?

When drawing your life curve, you have a number of possibilities:

- You could sketch a general life curve that depicts your whole life in one go.
- If it seems more meaningful to you, draw two curves, one for your feelings about your personal life and another, in a different color, for your professional development (career), beginning with kindergarten and elementary school.
- Once you have drawn your curve, list alongside it, in a series of bullet points, what it was that motivated you or demotivated you in any given situation.

Life's different periods

As already mentioned in the introduction, we go through different phases and crises in life. Life does not progress like a Gaussian curve – smoothly to a certain climax and then downhill until a natural end is reached in the form of death. This is neither the norm

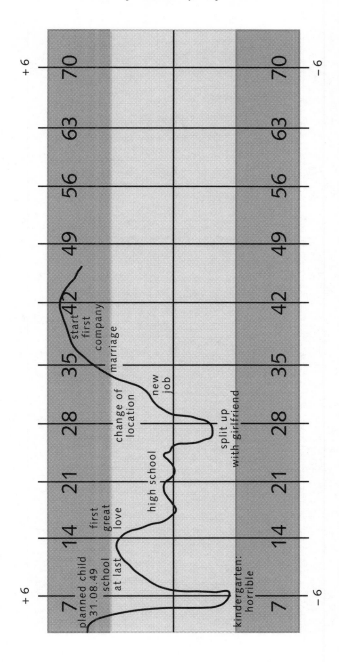

+6

+6

70 63 56 49 42 35 28 21 14 7

70 63 56 49 42 35 28 21 14 7

-6

-6

start
first
company

marriage

change of
location

new
job

high school

split up
with girlfriend

first
great
love

planned child
31.08.49
school
at last

kindergarten:
horrible

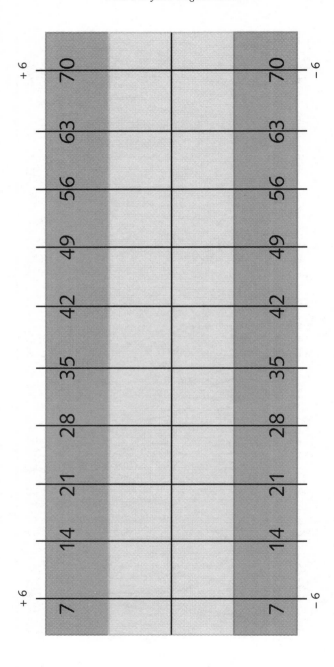

nor a foregone conclusion. There are plenty of happy and successful seniors just as there are despairing and unhappy teenagers or forty-somethings. Life doesn't follow a predictable pattern!

Let us assume that life progresses in seven-year periods. This number has by no means been chosen at random. It has always played an important role in human history. This symbolic figure even crops up in numerous places in the Bible (the seven days of creation, for example) and also occurs with conspicuous frequency in literature and history. Snow White with eight dwarves is as unthinkable as a list of six Wonders of the World.

Look at your life as a series of roughly seven-year periods. For example, in Germany, children start school at the age of six or seven. At 14 they may be confirmed (or, if not from a religious background, undergo the *Jugenweihe* initiation). By their early twenties these children will have finished school and completed military or community service or else will have taken their intermediate school certificate and completed their basic professional or vocational training. By 28, most students have completed their college or university studies. At 35 they will be in the middle of their professional careers and 42, for many, marks the start of the midlife crisis. In their mid-sixties they will reach retirement age and so on... Think about all the aspects of your life that follow a similar pattern.

Workshop: Previous periods in your life

In this workshop you will look at another chart which is also divided into seven-year segments. We invite you now to complete the challenging task of giving each section of your life to date a name. An example is shown on page 77.

For the periods that lie in the more distant past, this exercise is relatively easy, but the closer you get to the present day, or obviously if the seven-year period extends into the future, the more difficult it becomes to think of something concrete as a description. It is important to try, though. If you don't manage to attach a meaningful description to each period, you will at least realize that you urgently need to think more closely about this unclear section of your life. Where this happens, leave the relevant section of your lifeline empty and when you have finished reading the remaining chapters of this book, see if you can fill the gaps with life!

First of all, mark the stage you have currently reached. Then give each of the previous periods a name. Think about which period you enjoyed the most and what you want to achieve in the next seven-year period.

My educational history

As I follow the development of my children as a father, I gradually become more aware of all the things I have learned in my life, from handicrafts in elementary school to a rock 'n' roll course at secondary school and business English at university. What have you learned during your life? What courses have you completed and what further education have you undertaken? What did you find fascinating about it? The history of your education is also an important part of the puzzle where your potential is concerned.

Example of a 35-year-old man

Workshop: My educational history

To start with, here's an example:

Date	Form of education	Skills/ qualification/ title acquired	Comments
1950–54	Elementary school		
1954–64	High school theater group	School-leaving exams Amateur director	
1965–68	Bank training		Banker
1968–69	Community service (as alternative to military service)		
–1970	Training as voluntary worker at parish level	Basic training	Choirmaster

Now fill out the following table to help you think carefully about your own educational history.

Date	Form of education	Skill/ qualification/ title acquired	Comments

Books, people, films

You will have been influenced during the course of your life by many things, good and bad. These things contribute to your uniqueness. Many of them you have chosen specifically because they correspond to the way you are; others have entered your life unbidden but have left their mark on you nevertheless. Formative influences of this kind are often the focus of attention in any examination of "vocation" and are used as a basis for drawing conclusions about the future. They represent an important piece of the puzzle (though not the only one). What are the things that have particularly fascinated you and affected you in your life?

Books

What did you enjoy reading as a child? What particularly appealed to you about these books? Five people who read the same book will all be affected by it in a different way. We humans are very different from each other, and this is particularly evident in our reading habits. While one of my sons pores over non-fiction books for hours on end, the other is fascinated by an elite team of investigators (the *Five Friends*) who solve the trickiest of crimes together. Still others come into their own reading comics with speech bubbles. The much-adapted saying "show me the reading matter and I'll show you the man" is only partly exaggerated.

What books have you read? How has this influenced the way you think? Here we don't mean the set books you had to read at school – unless these made a particularly great impression on you.

Films

We are also fascinated by the most different movies. While some of us wait longingly for the next *Star Wars* sequel, others love films in which a heroic American president saves mankind single-handedly or a pair of lovers end up in each other's arms after numerous twists and turns.

Speeches, talks, ideas

Which sermons, talks and conversations do you remember? One of the most influential preachers in my life was my mother. She not only went through the Sunday sermons preached by our parish priest with us after church, but also guided me through everyday life in a way that made it easier for me to find the right direction in life. I remember listening as a teenager to a sermon in church on the Biblical story of the Good Father and realize now that this story, in conjunction with a book by Henry Nouwen, made a great impression on me. Another person whose views and ideas have benefited me greatly are those of my beloved wife. No one else can preach with such expertise and with personal relevance for me.

Others feel that the outlook and views of someone famous they respect can help them, and try to imagine how X, Y or Z would have reacted in the particular situation in which they find themselves. Which speeches, talks or lectures by professors or contemporaries have influenced you, even if this was just during a specific phase of your life?

Daytime and nighttime dreams

Dreams – daydreams as well as nighttime dreams – have been a major source of inspiration for many people. What dreams can you remember? Because we humans are all so different, different too are the formative influences on our lives. For a lot of people, dreams play a central role. Have you had dreams that have made such a strong impression on you that you can still remember them today?

Want

Another important factor is the strong effect that poverty and deprivation can have on us when we come into contact with them. Here is an example. A wealthy businessman sought out a counselor. He had already spent a lot of money on therapy but this had not cured his problem. In his opinion, he was "excessively" affected whenever he saw photographs, television reports or posters showing deprived children. He was even, on many occasions, moved to tears. He described this as "highly inopportune." Frequently, while on his way somewhere with business associates, he would see a poster of this kind and would be greatly upset by it. His first attempt to deal with the problem was to try to suppress these feelings. This didn't help. His second attempt consisted of working through his childhood with the help of a psychiatrist. He experienced many positive changes as a result, but none that really resolved the original problem. Finally, in his quest for a solution, he came across a counselor who thought his problem might have something to do with a sense of vocation.

They decided to conduct an experiment. The "patient" flew out to a third-world country for a couple of weeks to help nuns distribute soup to street children. Upon his return, this previously highly motivated businessman announced to his shocked family and bewildered colleagues that he had finally found his vocation and wanted to sell up and help the needy. The services of the counselor were called upon again, this time by his employers. Despite a careful search for someone to succeed this man, no suitable candidate had been found. The man's family approved of his decision in principle, but couldn't contemplate moving to another country.

After much give and take, a good compromise was reached. The man would continue to work for the same company for three weeks every four alongside his highly motivated team and channel a large part of the profits into projects aimed at helping needy children. He would spend an average of one week a month in different countries using this money to establish poverty-relief schemes.

We would now like to ask you to think about the issue that had tormented this businessman. Do you care deeply about any particular causes? Children with cancer, animal welfare, women's rights…? What are the areas to which you repeatedly feel you would like to make a commitment?

We would like to offer one piece of advice about the table on page 85. This table, which is for you to fill in with the things that have left a mark on your life, makes no claims to completeness. We have therefore supplied two empty categories in which you can add anything else you feel is an important influence on your life. For some this might be a proverb or saying; for others a verse from the Bible. Others might use this space for "prophetic words" – things other people have said that have had a profound effect on the way they think about the course they wish their lives to take.

Workshop: Formative influences

The table below lists books, films, speeches and talks, people and dreams. Of course, you can add any other categories that are particularly important in your life. Here's a tip: if you find it easier, you could start by listing all the individual things that occur to you and analyze them later. Here too we would like to offer an example:

Category	Title/author	What impressed you in particular?
Books	Karl May	A man who finds himself in a group of friends who have fallen out mediates and builds bridges between cultures (Winnetou).
	Tom Peters	Management can be fascinating!
Films	Regarding Henry	Embark on something new; free oneself from bad situations.
Speeches, talks	Martin L. King "I have a dream"	Fighting and dying for a dream and for justice. Dreaming of change and doing something about it.
People, encounters	Don Bosco	Building something up from nothing.
Dreams	I dreamed I was captain of a "dream ship."	As boss, making people happy in an inspiring environment.

Category	Title/author	What impressed you in particular?
Books		
Films		
Speeches, talks		
People, encounters		
Dreams		

Quality of life through forgiveness

When examining the past in depth, strange and unwelcome emotions can sometimes creep up on us as we revive certain memories. What would you say if you bumped into a certain old colleague in the street? Would you cross to the other side of the road?

Don't drag any unnecessary burdens from the past around with you. Of course it takes two to make a relationship work, but have you done everything you can on your side to end a difficult situation in a conciliatory manner? One of the most widely known prayers in the world, the Lord's Prayer, reminds us to forgive those who have done us wrong just as we ourselves need forgiveness for all the wrong we do. Of course this will not automatically lead to reconciliation. Reconciliation always takes two. But what part can you play in bringing it about?

Perhaps your father didn't send you greetings on your birthday. Don't burden yourself with things that are too big and too heavy for you to carry around and that impair your quality of life unnecessarily. Send him a nice card on his birthday wishing him many happy returns of the day. The rest is up to him.

Year in, year out, a large chain of stores receives anonymous letters containing sums of money from people who at some time in the past have taken something without paying for it. Clearly their consciences trouble them until they feel they have to make amends. The company donates all this money towards a good cause.

It is often the case that due to an old conflict we take a different route, out of defiance, to the one we really want to take. Organize your relationships proactively. You are only responsible for *your* part, but you are responsible for it fully and completely! Many a stupid word or deed cannot be undone, but we can at least be wise enough to admit to the other person that we were wrong. Every large stationer's sells attractive cards with the word "Sorry" printed on the front. The ability to admit their own mistakes is an important trait of mature people with strong characters. No one is perfect, and everyone knows that, so you don't need to pretend to be the only person in the world who is.

If you find that old wounds reopen while you are thinking this through, we would advise you to get help. A lot of people have been helped by a good counselor or therapist. You don't need to interrupt the process of this book over it, but don't let false pride rob you of your quality of life either!

Workshop: Life's impediments

1. What things, relationships, incidents are there in my life that need working through?

   _____

   _____

   _____

2. What occurs to me spontaneously as a way of dealing with these situations (e.g. "send a conciliatory card to Aunt Eugenie")?

   _____

   _____

   _____

Here too is an example:

Mistakes, strained relationships	What I contributed to this	Ideas about how to remedy the situation	When?
Sister-in-law	called her a stupid cow in the heat of the moment	send "Sorry" card	this evening
Peter	mistrust because I caught him fiddling his travel expenses	conversation – talk things over	next week

Mistakes, strained relationships	What I contributed to this	Ideas about how to remedy the situation	When?

What lies within you

Other people have left their mark on us and have thus contributed to creating our potential. In this section we will examine more closely what lies inside us that we can use in our life and career planning.

What do I enjoy doing? Motivating factors

Say your boss comes up to you at your desk tomorrow and announces that in future you will be getting an extra $1,000 in your monthly pay packet. How long, on average, do you think the motivation from a salary increase of this kind lasts? In our seminars, the reaction to this question is extremely varied. Some say a year, others six weeks. A study has reached the astonishing conclusion that, assuming we are talking about a living wage, the motivation created by a salary increase lasts no longer than 14 days on average. What, then, does motivate us?

The American scientist Arthur Miller has discovered that each of us is motivated by between seven and ten different factors that seem to be innate. For example, if presenting information is one of the motivating factors in your life, this activity itself will be a source of enjoyment to you and you will be able to practice it in a wide variety of different careers – taking a particular pleasure in it wherever you do so.

Most people spend their whole lives using the skills they learned early on in life. These may also be their motivating factors, but this is not automatically the case. Nevertheless, we prefer to stick to these areas because we are familiar with them. We favor familiar suffering over unfamiliar happiness – people can get used to almost anything. Do you know how certain Indian peoples train working elephants? Young animals are tethered to concrete blocks with a heavy chain and tempting items of food are placed on the ground just out of their reach. Naturally the hungry elephant tries to reach the food and pulls on the chain. The chain cuts into its flesh, inflicting a larger and larger wound and greater and greater pain. After a while, instead of being secured with a chain and a concrete block, the fully grown elephant can be tied to a stake in the ground with a simple rope and will no longer even think about escaping.

Perhaps your parents enjoyed doing a specific activity and thought you would at some point too. Even if you don't, we still remain faithful to what we know. There is no contradiction here with the workshops you have already completed in this book. Yes, you have been greatly influenced by your ancestors, but this influence should not be allowed to become a corset. Don't do things just because they met with approval during your childhood. Where necessary, liberate yourself from the guidelines laid down for you by those who brought you up.

However, let's not underestimate the qualities that are passed on to us by our home backgrounds. Those who grew up in a farming environment might have difficulty throughout their entire lives with intellectual work because life on the farm was all about performing physical tasks, using one's hands, mowing the meadow, milking the cows. Taking up a newspaper or book was a luxury that was possible at best during the winter months. Of course, the

reverse is true too. The professor's daughter who was constantly encouraged to learn languages and read books in her early years may find it difficult doing practical, physical work even if she has a strong interest in doing it. Free yourself from this inherited burden if you feel you want to try different areas of work!

What do you really like doing? What makes your eyes light up with enthusiasm? We all possess a wealth of abilities. Paul Ch. Donders and Michaela Kast, who developed the concept of *Creative Life Planning*, divide these abilities into four groups:

1. Ability with people
2. Ability with information
3. Ability with materials
4. Creative ability

Everybody should spend at least ten percent of their time doing things associated with their motivating factors. This is supposed to provide enough motivation for 100 percent of what they do. The closer their professional career corresponds to their motivating factors the better. I spend at least 60 percent of my time on things that are related to my motivating factors. I'm extremely fortunate!

When I was coaching at an Austrian convent, a nun of around 80 years of age came up to me and said: "You're so right about motivation!" Until ten years ago she had run a large kitchen. Out of the blue it was decided that she was now too old for the job and she was banished to the order's old people's home, where she was supposed to let herself be cared for. Within eight weeks she became very seriously ill. A wise new principal made it possible for her to carry on cooking for her fellow nuns several times a week and she returned to good health. Naturally there were a number of factors at play here, but one of them was definitely motivation. This nun is not an exception!

Is it not the case that our system of forcing people into retirement robs them from one day to the next of something essential in their lives? On the whole our society tends to hold older people in low esteem, which is why no one likes to be referred to as old (today even 70-year-olds insist that they are not old). This is a cultural problem inherent in our Western society. American psychologist Ellen J. Langer has shown that the Chinese have a completely different view of old age – with the result, for example, that the capacity of older Chinese people to remember details and experiences hardly differs from those of other age groups. In European and American culture, on the other hand, we positively expect people to become forgetful in old age and so they do (we are deliberately leaving real illnesses, such as Alzheimer's, out of the equation here). Orient your life according to your motivating factors, not your age! And act too on the assumption that you will continue to grow and try out new things beyond the age of 65.

The managing director of a very successful medium-sized business came to us with an urgent need for counseling. He had a more than satisfactory turnover, a loving wife and healthy children. At the start of the session, however, he described at length his desperate situation. If it weren't for his faith and his family, he declared, he would be in danger of committing suicide. When asked, cautiously, what he enjoyed doing, nothing occurred to him. So when was the last time he had had fun? Another long silence – there was nothing he could think of, nothing. After careful, repeated probing, something suddenly came to him: he described how he had constructed a dolls' house for his daughter full of realistic details – furniture, electric lighting and even a working shower for the dolls... The man came to life and his eyes lit up – it was hard to believe this was the same person who had seemed so depressed only moments before!

The context gradually became clear. The man had been an extremely talented carpenter. His customers were enthralled by his creative, cleverly constructed and high-quality "eco-furniture" and his fame spread throughout the country. He had to recruit more workers. Big corporations wanted to buy his unusual range. Soon he had over 40 employees, a full order book and fantastic margins. There was no end in sight to the firm's growth. He spent his time traveling from place to place negotiating new framework agreements or managing his permanently expanding business.

Pondering his situation, we realized that his current work as managing director had very little to do with the motivating factors in his life. He worked long and hard and his head found everything he did logical and good. But his heart missed the actual work of producing the furniture, handling the wood, designing and working on new models. He did not want to relinquish the firm. Besides, his position and relationships with customers couldn't be handed over to someone else just like that.

We therefore agreed a compromise. Every Tuesday he would pull on his overalls, enter the workshop and be given a job to do by the relevant foreman. We also consulted the foreman on this, who was thrilled by the idea. Since then the man has been working with wood every Tuesday and declares this to be his most fulfilling day's work. He also performs his management responsibilities well even though they are not the motivating factors in his life. What's more, he gets through the same amount of work as before, but with much more satisfaction and enjoyment.

In many businesses, good workers get promoted. The Peter Principle, named after the Canadian sociologist, Dr. Laurence Johnston Peter, who coined the phrase in his book of the same name, states that individuals get promoted until they reach a stage beyond the job they are qualified to do. To put it more bluntly: people climb the ladder until they are unable to do their job. They are unable to prove themselves in that position and so progress no further. A similar thing often occurs where motivating factors are concerned. One job suits an employee's talents perfectly, but the next highest position demands completely different qualities. If the employee is promoted he or she might enjoy more prestige and a higher salary, but these things alone do not make people happy in the long term.

In corporations that have taken account of this dynamic, we have frequently seen a dramatic improvement in levels of motivation. In one firm, a passionate salesman had to spend hours completing paperwork after every client meeting. While his sales record was unsurpassed, his administrative skills left a lot to be desired. His colleague, on the other hand, hated customer contact but was excellent at drawing up contracts and plans. The head of the company was considering getting rid of both of them, but could find no suitable replacements. At our suggestion the two joined forces: the salesman sold, an interface was organized, and his colleague did all the paperwork with great enthusiasm and to the highest possible standard. The sales commission was split between them. Turnover grew and both employees were happy.

The motivating factors of any given individual are distributed in such a way that they cannot all be realized through our jobs – a clear indication that we humans are not made for work alone. Many people make use of the same motivating factors in their leisure time that they use for work, albeit without the pressure (an important factor!) Others, however, organize their leisure time in such a way that it brings into play the motivating factors that are left over, those they cannot use at work.

A woman of around 50 discovered during a seminar that her dream and one of the motivating factors in her life was ballet and dance. During counseling she almost broke down in tears as she realized that this desire had lain dormant inside her for years. Her mother had talked her out of a career as a dancer, saying that she was too fat and that her dancing was terrible. So she had repressed the desire. Now she discovered that it was her absolute number one motivating impulse. It might have been too late to switch careers, but every Wednesday since the seminar she has been clearing her living room furniture aside, putting a good CD on the player and dancing through her apartment. This has become her most important appointment of the week.

A small tip for mothers (and fathers too, of course): we know today how important the presence of a parent is in bringing up children. Many mothers possess those motivating factors (compassion and the ability to communicate, for example) that go extremely well with the tasks of full-time mother and housewife. Others are also good housewives and model mothers, but the motivating factors in their lives lie in different areas (using computers, perhaps). This often leads to unnecessary frustration. Those who understand this will try to build their motivating factors into their routines. A full-time mother fascinated by computers and all their possibilities could, for example, do her household shopping on the internet instead of struggling through the supermarket with her small children.

What do you enjoy doing? Plan it into your life. We achieve more if we are motivated – professionally as well as privately! Combine your tasks proactively.

Workshop: What motivates me?

What are the motivating factors in your life? How can you find out? Sit down quietly and think about the things you passionately and repeatedly enjoy doing. Tell your partner or a friend three to five stories about things you have done with huge enthusiasm. Ask the person with whom you are discussing these stories to make a note just of the verbs you use.

From the incomplete list below, choose the motivating factors that might apply to you. Add any further skills you can think of.

People

1. Following instructions
2. Serving
3. Showing compassion, sympathy
4. Communicating
5. Convincing
6. Negotiating, making decisions
7. Establishing, building up
8. Handling
9. Advising
10. Teaching
11. Leading
12. _____

Information

1. Administration
2. Working out, calculating
3. Sorting things out
4. Investigating, researching
5. Evaluating, assessing
6. Organizing
7. Improving, adapting
8. Thinking logically
9. Planning, developing
10. Structuring, ordering
11. Developing concepts
12. _____

Materials

1. Processing
2. Working with the soil and nature
3. Using machines and tools
4. Using computers

Creative work

1. Performing, entertaining
2. Making music
3. Sculpting
4. Dancing
5. Miming

Materials	Creative work
5. Precision work	6. Acting
6. Building	7. Drawing
7. Painting and decorating	8. Designing
8. Repairing	9. Writing
9. Making table decorations etc.	10. Thinking creatively
	11. Photography
10. Working with electronics	12. _____
11. Cooking, baking	
12. _____	

Source: Paul Ch. Donders, "Kreative Lebensplanung," [A Creative Plan for Life] *Asslar 1997.*

What do you enjoy doing? What fulfils you?

Motivating factors	Where?	Why?	How can I enjoy this more often?
Making table decorations etc.	At home	Enhances enjoyment of life	By designing a "decoration of the month"

Get to know yourself

Everyone is unique. We know this to be true in theory, but what does it mean in practice? We are clearly identifiable from our fingerprints, and even more so from our genes. There is currently a debate going on as to whether this information should even be incorporated into passports and identity cards.

Your voice is also unique. Difficult as it may be for us to distinguish a mother from her daughter on the telephone, for example, this is perfectly simple for a computer, which can recognize your unique voice profile. Systems of this kind are already being used by the American army and also by various secret services.

In addition to external differences, we humans also have unique personalities. We pigeonhole people within the first 20 seconds of observing them. It is normal for us to attempt to analyze and categorize people according to the criteria with which we are familiar. We apply frameworks of this kind unconsciously in order to orient ourselves and make ourselves feel secure. Our tip: when you compartmentalize people in this way at least leave the compartment open! Your life could be enriched by the uniqueness of many different people, but prejudice – a judgement made before you truly know and understand the other person – often ends a relationship before it has really begun.

Over the next few pages we will introduce you to a tried and tested personality model designed to help you clarify the strengths and weaknesses of your own personality. It is fascinating to discover that many of your weaknesses are the flip sides of your strengths! The personality model in question is of the DISC type. The four letters in this acronym stand for four basic personality types: Dominant, Initiating, Stable and Conscientious. The DISC personality profile is widely used in staff recruitment. But it can also be used by private individuals who want to find out more about their own personalities. Let us simplify this complex area somewhat before making further distinctions.

Have you ever come across a truly extrovert individual? Conspicuous, communicative, self-assured, goal-oriented… What a contrast with the quiet, inconspicuous, possibly shy and reserved introverted type. If you had to assess yourself on a scale of one to ten, would you describe yourself as more introvert or extrovert under normal circumstances? Where do you feel most comfortable? Only a few people would classify themselves as one or ten. Can you see a bias in yourself one way or the other?

Naturally it depends to a great extent on surroundings. We held a coaching session with a group of five board members of the same corporation. One was more extrovert than the others. I don't think I have ever in my whole life encountered such a concentration of extrovert qualities. One member of the group was a tiny bit less conspicuously endowed in this area. As a result of comparing himself with the others, he considered himself to be highly introverted. During a break we visited his department. A member of staff who knew what we were doing there took me to one side and said: "Don't believe him when he claims to be introvert. I don't know the other board members, but he is the most extrovert individual I have ever set eyes on." So your surroundings can greatly affect the way you see yourself.

A commonly expressed theory in the 1970s was that we come into the world as a "blank sheet," our personalities being formed by the family home, our environment and other similar factors. Today this way of seeing things has changed. No one questions the powerful influence exerted by the past and one's environment, but it seems nevertheless that we have a core personality that is innate and unchangeable.

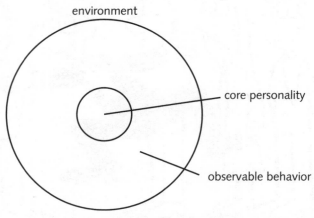

Core personality and observable behavior

"Shall we go jogging for half an hour?" A businesswoman married to an introverted man told us that upon returning to their car 27 minutes later, her husband carried on jogging around the parked vehicle for another three minutes. When she asked why he was doing that he replied: "We said we were going to run for half an hour."

I'm sure you wouldn't have any problem classifying this fellow as a typical representative of group C.

Had our businesswoman been married to an extroverted and people-oriented man, he would no doubt have become engaged in an in-depth conversation with a passer-by as soon as they had got out of the car. The planned half-hour would have disappeared in a

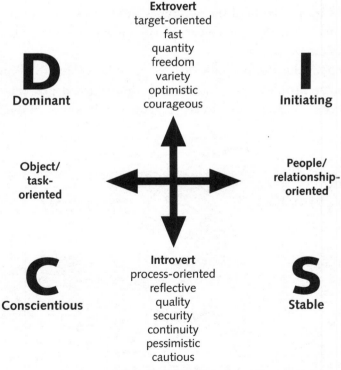

The characteristics of the DISC personality types

flash, his next appointment would already be pressing and the jogging would have fallen by the wayside once more. Behavior of this type can be clearly classified under "I" on the chart.

Extrovert people generally do things at a fast pace while introverts tend to be slower. Try surprising both types with the request for a decision regarding some new matter and observe which of them finds it easier to reach a quick decision. Real extroverts generally attain goals quickly. They tend to be more eloquent, more open, louder and faster.

In addition to the significant difference between extroverts and introverts, people can either be object/task-oriented or people/relationship-oriented. While the first like to perform tasks alone, the second prefer to work with other people. Naturally some people are a mixture of the two types and like to combine both in their lives. Which gives you more enjoyment? Decide which one applies to you!

To sum up: the purpose of these profiles is not to compartmentalize people and so block their thinking and prevent them from ever escaping from "their" pigeonhole. It is more a question

the ideal job

of helping us to exploit our strengths in a carefully targeted way or to develop a knowledge of our own weaknesses so that we can exercise more caution in certain situations. The better our individual strengths are adapted to the life situation in question, the more effective and fulfilled our lives will be. People who like to take the initiative, for example, will be uncomfortable working for any length of time for a company that is run in an authoritarian manner. For them, taking the (carefully considered and well thought-out) step of working for themselves can be a liberating experience. Those who know themselves better will also know that by working in the right field they will be able to achieve more.

Workshop: My personality structure

Although the following table is not a full DISC profile, it nevertheless demonstrates what use a personality profile of this type can serve. You can find out more about the method by visiting www.disg.de.

Please read carefully through all the adjectives (results-oriented, decisive etc.) in the right-hand column of the table and mark the statements that apply to you.

Dominant	• Strengths	• results-oriented • decisive • likes challenges • independent • sets the ball rolling • teamwork: driving force that shows way ahead • in a management role: gets things moving, manages problems and unrest
	• Weaknesses	• impatient • not good at contact with others • poor listener • can make hasty decisions • difficult team worker • demands too much of others • overlooks risk
	• Ideal working environment	• freedom to make decisions • challenges • large projects • working alone • as little control as possible • as little detailed work as possible • clear goals
Initiating	• Strengths	• good at forging contacts • radiates optimism and enthusiasm • knows how to enjoy life • good and enthusiastic communicator • creates a motivating atmosphere • teamwork: good at establishing contact • in management role: facilitates open communication, looks for consensus over ultimate decisions
	• Weaknesses	• recognition-dependent • disorganized • shuns confrontation • fails to see things through to the end • talks too much • can work poorly by self • insufficient attention to accuracy
	• Ideal working environment	• variety • people • time to enjoy life • as little detailed work as possible • flexible conditions • opportunity to communicate • public recognition

The four main DISC types

Stable	• Strengths	• creates harmony • good team worker • good listener • loyal • creates a stable environment • teamwork: ensures harmony, performs specialized tasks • in management role: helps others do their work
	• Weaknesses	• indecisive • cannot say "no" • too defensive • shuns argument • over-readiness to compromise • too quick to set aside own wishes • copes badly with change
	• Ideal working environment	• security, stability • time to adjust to change • teamwork • recognition of self • clear expectations • harmonious environment • good, clear relationships
Conscientious	• Strengths	• love of detail • quality-conscious • thinks critically, analyzes • sees things through • pays attention to rules and norms • teamwork: concentrates on important details • in a management role: places an emphasis on completion of tasks; requires procedures to be followed
	• Weaknesses	• gets bogged down in detail • tendency towards perfectionism • danger of withdrawing into role of mere observer • too much emphasis on "doing things properly" • insufficiently flexible • takes too long to make decisions • pessimistic
	• Ideal working environment	• clear expectations • rules, norms • reasons given for change • recognition for work done • clear description of tasks • opportunity to ask questions • tasks that require precision

Continuation: the four main DISC types

Leading a valuable and value-led life

What are you prepared to spend money on? If you ask a number of different people this question, the range of replies you receive will astonish you – and this is good. We all have a different set of things that are valuable to us, a kind of personal value profile. No doubt you and your friends will have a certain number of values in common. If, however, your value profile is absolutely identical to that of those around you, either you don't know yourself very well or else you have relinquished a part of your essential individuality.

Every individual has personal as well as social values, all of which are subject to change. The stability of our personal values increases as we get older. The influence of these values on our decision-making is far greater than was previously thought. It is of comparable importance to that of personality and individual aptitudes.

This is not by any means restricted to our private lives. More and more specialists are recognizing the enormous influence of our value profiles on our behavior and decision-making in our professional lives. This dynamic is being recognized by an increasing number of corporations and is also being integrated into the way businesses are managed. Many firms even stipulate value compatibility as a precondition for collaboration with other companies: "If you want to supply us, the same values that are important to us must be important to you." Values are to people what an operating system is to a computer. Far more of what we do is based on our values than we are aware of.

Here is a real-life example. Despite quality checks on outgoing goods, a manufacturer had a high level of returns of defective products. Its customers were dissatisfied and the reactions of both press and market were threatening business. When the problem was analyzed more closely, it was discovered that the management had instituted the following as its motto: "We must produce larger quantities of our products in significantly less time." The line speed was increased considerably and the guidelines set out for individual processes were breathtaking. All the workers were doing their best, but after a while they just became frustrated. The management was still not aware of this. Combined with an authoritarian style of management that meant employees were publicly reprimanded for making mistakes, this situation led to a spectacular increase in defective production.

Mistakes were concealed and, for reasons of cost control, quality checks were reduced to random sampling. This was carried out under the absurd slogan: "Cost what it may, we will reduce costs." Quality and other values were mere paper promises. "Bean-counters" took short-sighted decisions.

What counts is not what is written down on paper, but what is put into practice. I repeatedly encounter businessmen who want to know: "How can I get my staff to put into practice something I, as boss, don't practice myself?" Ploys of this kind only work in the very short term. Guardini says that preaching is 10 percent words, 30 percent deeds and 60 percent the example we set by our own behavior. The greater the stress, the more we reveal of who we are and what is really important to us. This influences our surroundings and preaches considerably louder than either words or deeds. Our values are an important part of the message we convey. Our values can influence a relationship, an organization, our entire surroundings.

This means that people's values should be taken into account as an important factor. There is a saying in American business: "Because of competence you hire, because of character you fire!"

What are your values? What are healthy values for a company? This leads to further questions: how can I lead my life in a way that truly corresponds to my values? How can I make my staff act in accordance with our corporate values? Are the staff even compatible with these values in the first place?

If not, depending on how important your values are to your company, this will repeatedly create problems. Staff will act according to their own values and behave as they see fit. If their values correspond to those of the company and also those of your customers, then you have won. The greater the level of stress, the more clearly their values will come to the fore.

We are convinced that there are a number of basic values – principles that allow our lives to function as they should and that are essential to peaceful coexistence with others. It is important to know what these are and to incorporate them into our own lives.

If these basic values are not present in a relationship, organization or culture, disaster will ensue. Human rights are a good example of this. Following a very liberal period, we believe we are now able to discern a growing awareness of the importance of values and that increasing numbers of people are prepared to incorporate values into their lives and organizations. We hope this trend continues.

A society, an organization, advertising – they all, in their way, have a "missionary" purpose and stand for specific values. Not all values are workable, and some can even be destructive. A business can have good values and operate by them, but its value profile may nevertheless be incompatible with your own. The term used for this is a clash of values. Tensions in teams and relationships can frequently be traced back to different values or a different prioritization of values.

For me, continuing education and personal development are extremely important values that have become stronger and stronger over the years. They are things I stand up for and promote in word and through the way I lead my life. In addition to my main career I have an executive role in a particular organization. I could almost have destroyed this organization as a result of mistakenly believing that all the organization's members had to share the same values. After much tension we finally worked out a common value profile for the organization and I was made aware of how easily we can succumb to the danger of projecting our values onto others. I make time to examine my value profile, reviewing it carefully and attempting to protect it from "viruses." Dream days provide a good framework for this too.

Is it possible for us to live with people with a different value profile to our own, to be married to them, for example? Yes it is, as long as the relationship is characterized by mutual respect (one of the basic values). Different value profiles are even the norm. An immature handling of the situation can lead to the danger of a struggle in which one party tries to force his or her own value system on the other. It often seems to me that smoothly running partnerships unconsciously develop a value profile of their own that is compatible, though not identical, with the value profiles of the individuals concerned.

Workshop: Clarification of personal values

This workshop will help you to identify your personal values. It will also help you to identify the areas you want to change. Using the table below, enter how important each of the values and relationships is to you and how important a place it currently occupies in your life. Where there are significant discrepancies, don't delay – decide today what you will do to remedy the situation!

How important to me is ...	Enter a score from 1–6 (1 = very important; 6 = not important)	What is the reality? from 1–6	Discrepancy	What am I going to do about it?
Example ...a good relationship with colleagues and family?	2	4	2	• Invite colleagues for tea • Hold get-togethers and celebrate minor successes; send positive memos • Praise a colleague every day

How important to me is ...	Enter a score from 1–6 (1 = very important; 6 = not important)	What is the reality? from 1–6	Discrepancy	What am I going to do about it?
1. ...a good relationship with colleagues and family?				
2. ...good standing at work?				
3. ...achievement of personal goals?				
4. ...capacity for teamwork and ability to work with others?				
5. ...leisure time and enjoyment?				
6. ...wealth and prosperity?				
7. ...health and fitness?				
8. ...making an important contribution to society?				
9. ...respecting other people's success				
10. ...independence, lack of ties and freedom to develop				
11. ...personal and intellectual growth (further education etc.)?				
12. ...time with family and close friends?				
13. ...career and professional challenges?				
14. ...responsible behavior?				
15. ...time for God and the search for meaning?				

What, then, are your own personal values? In the preceding exercise you entered a score for 15 different values. Take a closer look at the values you have identified as having the highest priority for you. Are these the values that reflect your own value system or are there others that play an important role in your life?

My values	How do I wish to live these values?
Example: Respecting other people's successes	• Listen more closely when people are reporting their successes • Send friendly memos congratulating people on their achievements
1.	
2.	
3.	
4.	
5.	
6.	
7.	
8.	

Second step:
Reorient your life

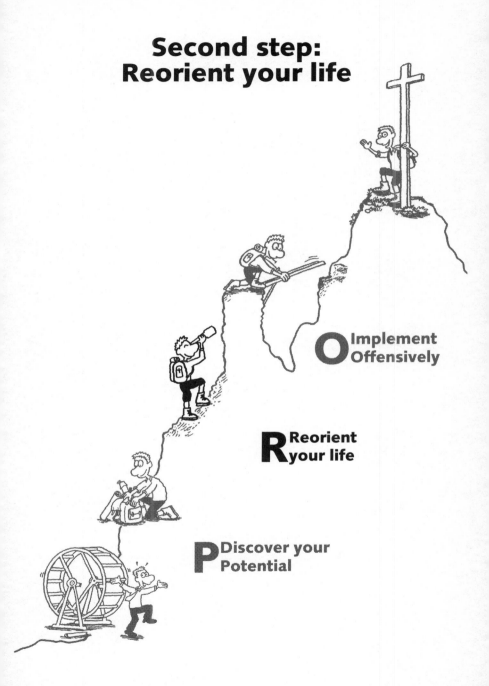

O Implement
Offensively

R Reorient
your life

P Discover your
Potential

Where there is no vision, the people perish.

Proverbs 29, 18

You have broken out of the hamster wheel. In the course of the preceding chapter you will have learned what lies within you and will now know exactly what your potential consists of. But doing an inventory of the larder does not necessarily mean you know what to cook. Your potential gives you an idea of the direction your life should take and how you might be able to get the best out of it.

The main purpose of the following chapter is to clarify what is meant by the enigmatic term *vision*. Vision has become a buzzword that is generally used in a rather abstract way. We want to rescue the word from the realm of the vague and incomprehensible. Your image of the future should acquire a more definite outline and become more colorful. You will have to take decisions even while painting this picture. In many cases, saying "yes" to one option in life often means saying "no" to others. A series of workshops will help you improve your feel for what is right for you. You will be able to reflect on and decide which path to the future you consider to be the best one.

The power of an inner model

All things are created twice: firstly as an idea and secondly as reality. Even the ancient Greeks were convinced of this. You may think it is self-evident, but it is something very few people make use of in their lives. A successful, fulfilled, happy life is not the product of random developments, but a reflection of the inner world of someone who has prepared for success, fulfillment and happiness and has consciously or unconsciously converted the corresponding ideas into reality. Naturally we know there are things we are incapable of influencing – strokes of fate, insidious illness, bad luck, global developments that we have no control over. But we can always influence what lies within us.

Imagine that today is a special day: at last you can move into your first ever custom-built house. An urgent business trip has meant that you have spent the last few weeks abroad and a removals firm has packed up your entire belongings and unpacked them again in your new house. You drive up full of excitement – your house! You stand in front of the entrance and carefully compare the reality with your plans. Next you are surrounded by your own four walls, see your familiar furniture in unfamiliar rooms and again compare what has been achieved with your mental picture, a picture that took shape in your mind's eye over the course of countless evenings…

When did you start to build your house? No, I don't mean the day the excavator came and you celebrated the turning of the first sod with a few friends and a bottle of champagne. I mean how and when did the idea of your house first take shape? Perhaps it was like this: seven years ago you visited a friend who had just finished building his own house. Up to this point, you had never considered acquiring a house of your own, but then you experienced the atmosphere, the large rooms, the inspiring location, the effective lighting, the stylish furniture... To your spontaneous and jocular question of whether he might like to sell it to you, your friend replied: "You'll have to build a house of your own!"

From this point on, something changed inside you. All of a sudden you started to become aware of houses everywhere you went and soon began to take deliberate note of what was attractive and what was ugly about the different buildings you saw. Something began to take shape inside you – a mental image of "your" dream house. Then, three years ago, you visited your architect for the first time. You explained your ideas to him enthusiastically. Initially he reacted with some reserve and started to ask questions: whether you knew how much your ideas would cost, what financial resources you had at your disposal and so on. After agreeing on the appropriate dimensions, he set to work on the initial designs. It gave you a shock when he presented his ideas for the first time. What he had sketched out was not your house, it was his house! It was not the picture you had in your mind. How you wished back then that there had been some means of transmitting images directly, brain to brain – he could simply have downloaded your mental image and converted it into a plan...

All things that can be seen taking shape have an invisible beginning. You have an idea. A mental image begins to develop, initially vague but gradually it becomes more and more concrete. Usually this mental image is transformed during the development process. You have an image of your future, your life, your company, a highly specific task and even of your family. You can influence and shape this mental image. If you do not consciously shape this image, one will develop unconsciously that you will then work on implementing. These mental images are even stronger than the ideas you have set down on paper at some time or other. Mental images of things guide us forward and influence our behavior.

To live consciously and proactively means actively shaping this inner picture, continually revising and improving it. Intuition is not without its uses, but it is sometimes too capricious. It does not, as a rule, lead us firmly enough to where we want to be. This is why you need to go a decisive step further: actively shape your future! Don't let things just run their own course; add detail to the picture that will describe your future.

This mental image can also, of course, be called a vision, a model or a snapshot of the finish. Our inner model has enormous power and exercises immense influence over our lives. At the same time it is something living that has to be shaped and rethought, something that requires updates and upgrades. You will never achieve a "perfect" model if you are afraid of starting out with an incomplete test version.

We often find it difficult to develop a clear idea about our future life. Many people have a poor memory and find it hard to remember facts, names and arrangements. It is now known that memory, like musculature, can be trained. The same is true for creativity and the ability to think forward to the future. If you do not wish to be controlled by others, start to practice. Train yourself to think creatively about your future life. You will discover that it is easier than you think!

Finding a balance

Which area of your life did you think about just now when we were talking about visions? Your current employment, your entire life's work, your marriage? It is, of course, possible to achieve a synopsis of a life, but no one has just one vocation. We can have different vocations during different periods of our life, in different areas of life and so on. In a transcultural study, the psychiatrist and researcher Nossrat Peseschkian has shown that in order for our lives to develop healthily, we have to achieve a balance between four main areas:

1. *Self*: this covers our physical well-being, e.g. exercise, nutrition, relaxation.
2. *Achievement*: where would you like to exercise your capacity for work – professionally, privately or in a voluntary role?
3. *Relationships*: relationships are an important part of your life and your quality of life. How do you see the future unfolding for your relationship with your partner, your relationship with your own children, your relationship with your circle of friends?
4. *Meaning*: why do you do the things you do? If the first half of life is dominated by the issue of "having," during the second, more attention is paid to the question of "meaning." Wise men and women invest in this area of life regularly and in good time.

Confronted with these four points, most readers will feel they are still some way off achieving a balanced life. There are a number of industries that specialize in repairing the damage caused by a lack of balance in our lives. Are you under so much pressure that you are not eating properly? No problem, magazines that publish diets, food manufacturers that sell diet products and fitness studios will look after you...

Career-oriented people (men in particular) are all too quick to sacrifice relationships in order to get ahead in their jobs. As a rule it is the family that suffers most as a result. Many people only become aware of this when it is already too late. Whenever you find yourself facing an opportunity to get ahead in your career, stop to consider how much this will upset the balance of your life. Will you still be able to find time to have deep conversations with your partner? Will you only experience your children's development through the updating of the family photographs on your desk? It remains a fundamental truth that no career move is worth the destruction of a marriage. This principle needs to be acknowledged even by those who have fallen victim to an egotistical way of thinking for they are no more immune to serious crises in life – a

bad illness or unemployment, for example – than anyone else. Who will help them through such crises if not the partner they had planned to grow old with?

And people treat their bodies, souls and minds in a similarly unbalanced manner. Many cardiac and circulatory illnesses could be avoided if more attention were paid to exercise and nutrition. Even in demanding jobs, the mind can atrophy if it is fed only with technical or specialist subject matter. Delve into a challenging work of world literature once in a while! Learn a new language! Radically re-examine your views on God and the world!

As with relationships, it is true that we only become aware of our deficiencies during major life crises. If I define myself in terms of income alone, what will I do if I lose my fantastic job? How will I cope with the transition to retirement if work has been the only thing in my life?

The practices of doctors, psychotherapists and divorce lawyers offer daily proof that paying attention to the balance of our lives is by no means a luxury for people who enjoy brooding on such matters. On the contrary, a balanced life is essential if we do not wish to be swept away by some crisis or other. From personal experience, but also based on our encounters in seminars and coaching sessions, we can see clearly the devastating effect on people's lives of thinking that focuses on career alone.

Just to avoid any misunderstanding, we say yes to the achievement-oriented society and yes to top performance in the workplace. At the same time, however, we know that this kind of performance cannot be sustained while it results in an imbalanced life. A top manager who is off work for weeks on end because of a heart operation impresses us as little as a senior executive who performs her work "with the parking brake on" for several months while she is going through painful divorce proceedings.

It is important, therefore, that you do not lose this balance. We recommend in any case that you do not develop visions for the professional sphere alone. In order to live a healthy life in the long term, regular reflection and action are required in all the main areas of life.

Is having wishes the same as wishful thinking?

It is no accident that in fairy tales and legends, good fairies or genies are always popping out of bottles granting people wishes. We are all full of unfulfilled desires and wishes. "Happiness beyond desire" is a fiction. People without wishes are dead (or dishonest). Many people suffer from the very opposite: being driven by their desires and wishes without being able to simply enjoy the moment. What wishes and dreams do you have?

It is interesting that wishes play an important role even in ancient Biblical texts. Abraham, for example, wishes for a child and one of the Psalms of David includes the verse: "Delight thyself also in the Lord; and he shall give thee the desires of thine heart" (Psalms 37, 4). Naturally there are also destructive wishes, but there can be no doubt that a healthy relationship with one's desires and wishes definitely plays an important role in a fulfilled life.

What do you wish for? Whenever I ask my children what they would like, their eyes light up and they are seldom at a loss for an answer. Their horizons may be limited at the moment to toys and things they "want to have," but with a little practice they can be expanded. Ask children what they wish for – from their parents, politicians and society – from time to time. Some fascinating books of children's wishes have been published.

Sometimes it seems as if our ability to wish for things gets left behind with our childhood. This seems to be a cultural peculiarity of our society, for international workshops have shown that there are striking differences in this respect between nations. In Germany, people still philosophize about whether they should have wishes at all and how useful this is, while others have already drawn up long lists of their wishes. I repeatedly find that people are fearful of expressing wishes, and find that disappointment over unfulfilled wishes is the main argument against having them in the first place. However, if you have a bad experience with a particular dish, you don't normally give up eating altogether. For this reason we would like to encourage you to wish for things once more. In this section you can give free rein to your dreams – we'll return to Earth in the next chapter.

Workshop: What are my most important dreams and wishes?

Not every wish is there to be fulfilled. Many are and will remain dreams and that is fine! But what dreams lie dormant inside you – for your professional life, for people you would like to help, for your targets, ideas of things you wish to achieve?

Taking proper cognizance of our dreams is an important step. Not for nothing do psychologists regard an unhealthy relationship with our wishes and desires as a potential basis for addiction.

We would like to recommend that you follow the following steps:

1. On the table on page 126 list as many of your wishes as you can think of – from a new washing machine and that world trip to your dream career and ideal life.
2. Then use the analysis column to examine the background to these wishes. What pleasant feelings do you associate with a particular wish? If, for example, you have entered "wealth" as one of your

wishes, is this because you want to be independent of other people or because you want the privilege of being able to enjoy luxury?

Wish	What motivates you, appeals to you about this wish?

While you have just listed the wishes that have spontaneously occurred to you, you can now use the table on page 128 to embark upon a journey of discovery. Nine different areas of life are listed to help you also track down those wishes to which you pay less attention. The following example shows a number of possible wishes.

Area of life	Wish list
Family	– three lovely, healthy children – a wonderful spouse
Financial	– to be financially independent at 40 – to be very wealthy by the end of my life
Intellectual	– to have read the collected works of Shakespeare – to be familiar with all the major writers and thinkers
Sport	– to have run a marathon – to be fitter at 60 than I am today
Social	– to enjoy a good standing in society – to have lots of friends
Spiritual	– to have a firm belief in God – to understand Jesus Christ and his work better
Professional	– to make rapid and continuous progress – to enjoy my work
Leisure	– to have a fishing hut by a lake in Norway – to own a motor caravan in which to tour Europe
Sundry	– to have a dog – to own a large detached house – to own a Mercedes (S-Class) – to maintain good health – to go on a world trip

Area of life	Wish list
Family	
Financial	
Intellectual	
Sport	
Social	
Spiritual	
Professional	
Leisure	
Sundry	

If you would like to know how you really stand, complete the following workshop, which uses a knock-out system to highlight your real priority in life. Think of the dreams and wishes you listed on page 128 as being in competition with each other. Only one can win. Please note: it is not a question of playing off particular areas against one another (family against professional life, for example). It is a question of working out the following scenario: if push came to shove and for whatever reason you had to choose between two wishes – which would you opt for?

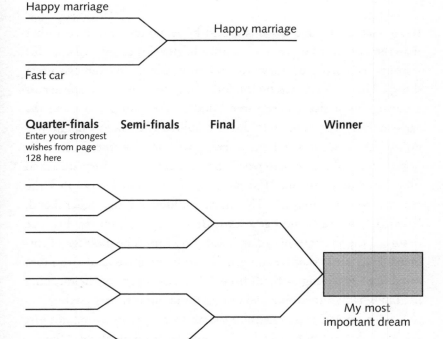

Happy marriage

Happy marriage

Fast car

Quarter-finals   **Semi-finals**   **Final**   **Winner**
Enter your strongest
wishes from page
128 here

My most
important dream

Living with goals – your snapshot of the finish

If your potential and dreams are to be exploited and lived rather than remain mere fantasies, they must be developed into visions, for visions also drive us forward and motivate us to achieve great things. This is illustrated by the following story. A man came across a construction site where three builders were all performing the same activity. He went up to the first builder and asked what he was doing. "As you can see, I am working with my hammer," came the bored reply. The man then went up to the second worker and asked him the same question. "I'm working on a pointed window," the fellow replied grumpily. The third builder, on the other hand, beamed: "We're building a cathedral!" The gleam in his eye betrayed the strength his great vision gave him. The message of this instructive tale is that we can only be truly effective (and also more capable of surviving difficult times) if we are aware of the meaning behind what we are doing and bear in mind our ultimate goal.

It is also possible to imagine a fourth worker who would not just see the cathedral, but also what it would mean to mankind. "We are working on something that will change our city and its people for ever," he might add, before going on to paint a picture in words of the effect the cathedral would have on the lives of the local people, the events that would be held there and how these would exert a positive influence over people and society near and far.

It's all a question of vision

What are you working on in your life? Your vision should be large and demanding! It should be related to your potential. Here too it is a matter of having the end in sight at the beginning. What do you want to have achieved by the end of your life?

Workshop: Snapshot of the finish – discovering your vision in life

Imagine you are celebrating your 85th birthday. Lots of relatives, friends and acquaintances have turned up for the occasion. A toast is drunk to you and there are various speeches in your honor. Your spouse steps forward to say a few words, as does your former boss, your children, a friend, a neighbor. What, in all honesty, would they say about you? In what way has your life stood out? If you are not married or have no children, simply replace these people with others who have played a key role in your life. Take a sheet of paper and draft out the different birthday speeches on it. You can, of course, use the table below if you prefer. It is helpful to formulate the statements first of all and then think about the values behind them.

You can also vary this exercise by imagining yourself in the following situation: it is not your 85th birthday but your funeral. People you have known step up and speak about what your life has meant. Describe in a series of bullet points what you think these people would say:

Person	Snapshot of the finish: what would you like these people to say?	What would they say if they were being honest?
Spouse or partner		

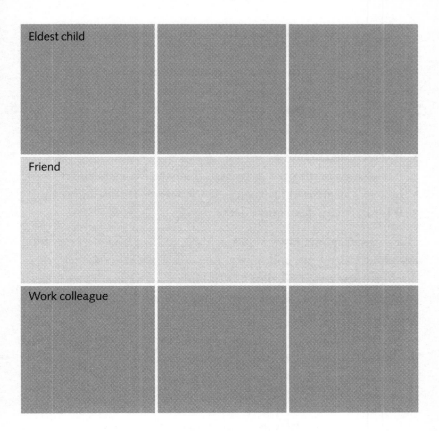

This exercise shows that it is far from easy to describe our future. Only if we succeed in doing so, however, can we determine our future ourselves. How can you transform the speeches you have noted down into a vision? Over the next few pages we will suggest three ways of going about this:

- By formulating your vision in words.
- By compiling a photograph album that contains pictures of your vision.
- By drawing your own picture (this is easier than one might imagine).

Capturing your vision in words

People who have difficulty visualizing things will no doubt find it easier to use words. Set down your vision in writing, bearing in mind the key elements of an appealing and energy-giving life vision:

- It is recorded in writing.
- It is written in the present tense as if it had already been achieved.
- It covers all areas of life such as work, family, leisure and so on.
- It is filled with descriptive detail.

Here's an example: my vision for life is to be a friend to my wife, my children and my colleagues. As such, I am there to help them discover their potential, develop and live. I jog at least twice a week so that I'll be fitter at 60 than I am today. I'll run at least two marathons in my life.

So, what is your vision for life? If you have decided on this method, set your vision down on a separate sheet of paper.

Your life in a photograph album

You might prefer to follow this second method and buy yourself a new photograph album. Collect articles, magazines, periodicals, photographs – anything that inspires you with regard to your future. Whenever you have time, for example on your next dream day, go through these documents and cut out anything that spontaneously appeals to you. Sort this material out and stick it into your photograph album in an ordered fashion. Begin, for example, with the subject House/Apartment then move on to Holidays/Travel; another area could be inspiring articles on the subject of relationships or how to lead a meaningful life.

If you have a lot of good individual dreams and wishes that cannot simply be joined together without further ado to form a large whole, try the following method:

- Buy yourself a simple scrapbook or album (these can be obtained cheaply from any department store).
- Collect old magazines, periodicals and catalogues.
- Call in at the travel agent's and pick up brochures for all the countries you are interested in.
- Whenever you have time (in the evening, during a break or on a dream day), go through these documents and cut out everything that spontaneously appeals to you.
- Sort out these pictures and texts by subject matter and stick them into your scrapbook.
- Begin with the subject House/Apartment, then move onto Holidays/Travel, Pets and so on.
- Review your scrapbook regularly. Whenever you come across a picture that depicts an aspect of your dream better than the existing one, use it to replace the old one.
- Gradually, all the different areas of your vision will become clearer and more colorful until at some point you will open the album and say to yourself: "That's exactly how I want my life to look one day!"

Your life as a map

Many people with a bias to the right side of the brain (those who work better with shapes, colors and emotions than with words and numbers), will find it easier to develop a snapshot of where they want to get to in life using a drawing. This kind of "map of one's own life" should flow naturally from the pen. Try to draw a picture. Let it develop in your mind and then transfer it to paper. By no means does it have to be a work of art, nor do its different elements have to be in proportion. It is more a question of sketching out the course of your life in a free and easy manner. If you are not a natural artist, you can use matchstick men or symbols. Drawing uses different parts of the brain and will allow you to become more aware of things than if you simply tried to wrap them up in words. Below is an example.

How visions mature

Visions grow and mature. They develop over the course of a life. We recommend that you review your vision regularly, at least once

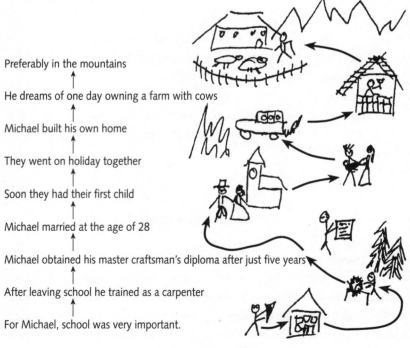

Preferably in the mountains

He dreams of one day owning a farm with cows

Michael built his own home

They went on holiday together

Soon they had their first child

Michael married at the age of 28

Michael obtained his master craftsman's diploma after just five years

After leaving school he trained as a carpenter

For Michael, school was very important.

A "map of your life"

a year. During numerous executive coaching sessions we have observed the positive dynamic that arises when instead of remaining one-off actions, visions are allowed to develop and mature.

History offers astonishing examples of how a vision has dictated the course of an entire life. Margaret Thatcher lived until the age of 21 above her father's grocery store. The story goes that she used to look out of the window at the people below and dream of one day entering politics on their behalf.

One autumn day, a young Italian named Adriano Olivetti stood in front of the Underwood plant in Connecticut/USA and stared at the red brick building. At this time Underwood was one of the largest and best-known typewriter manufacturers in the world. One day, he dreamed, he would own a factory like this and the name Olivetti would stand for the same quality as Underwood. 34 years later, Adriano returned to America and bought Underwood for 8.7 million dollars. His life's dream had come true.

We would not wish to conceal the fact that there can also be limits to dreams and visions. Here we would like to warn of the dangers of a false "everything is possible" attitude by which many motivational trainers have been infected. The saying "If you can dream it, you can do it" that is currently circulating in America is misleading in its absoluteness. A 60-year-old no longer has any chance of becoming a professional soccer player and in this respect has to accept his natural limitations. Failed visions can throw people who do not manage to achieve their goals in life (despite having ambitious dreams and working extremely hard to fulfill them) into self-doubt and can produce feelings of guilt. Outsize visions that are initially inspiring can turn out later to induce paralysis because the individual concerned feels in his heart of hearts that he can never fulfill his vision. This is not to say that large visions are necessarily bad, but it is worth remembering that the road to achieving them is stony and that the world can muster astonishing power in thwarting people's plans.

Your private constitution:
the mission statement

Agents are out there performing secret missions, diplomats are embarking on tricky assignments...and you too have a "mission." What is your role in life? What have you been equipped to do? You have already worked this out through an exploration of your dreams, visions and snapshots of the future. Formulating a mission statement has proved itself to be a useful way of turning all this into a basis for life planning.

A mission statement can best be compared to an article in the constitution of a nation or a federal state. Statements of this kind are often rather general and visionary, but set out a clear path for the future. Article 3 of the Basic Law (or constitution) of the

Federal Republic of Germany, for example, states that "Men and women shall have equal rights." This is certainly not a description of the current state of affairs across all areas of life, but it nevertheless represents a basis for legislation and state decision-making. Ultimately, everything that occurs within a nation has to be measured against its constitution. A new law that flouts an article of Germany's basic law can (and must) be declared null and void by the Federal Constitutional Court.

Write a "basic law" or constitution for your life. A mission statement:

- is an attempt to express your values and visions in an all-embracing key phrase
- is your motto and the basic principle by which you lead your life. Its purpose is to remind you in a succinct manner of your main values and goals in life
- provides orientation and motivation and expresses your life in a nutshell
- can exert a kind of control function over your time planning. If you spend time on things that stand in the way of your mission statement, they can be seen as "unconstitutional" with respect to your vision.

Here are a few examples of mission statements:

- Work: *I am one of the best in my chosen field both inside and outside my company. My commitment is a decisive factor in the success of my firm.*
- Marriage/relationship: *I confirm my choice of spouse/partner every day by showing my love for him/her in word and deed.*
- Whole life: *My mission is to act credibly and with integrity and to perceptibly improve the lives of other people.*

What would your mission statement look like? Write down what you want to bring about or achieve through your life, what benefit you wish to pass on. As a result of your actions, do you want to leave the world a slightly "better," a slightly "more worthwhile" place than when you entered it? What contribution would you like to make to your firm, to society, the church, your children? While going through this process, pay careful attention to your feelings. Psychotherapist Victor Frankl was of the conviction that we do not invent our "mission" in life, we track it down. In other words, what we regard as our task and goal in life is something that already exists inside us. All we have to do is uncover it and recognize it.

We know people who have devised a mission statement for each of the main areas of their lives and others who have one that covers their whole life. There is no right or wrong approach, although we would not recommend giving more than five to eight different areas of life a mission statement as the motivating effect is likely to be lost. You could, for example, write a mission statement for your professional life, your marriage, your family and any voluntary work you do.

For his marriage, a good friend adopted the motto: "My wife, my best friend." In his professional life he lived out the mission statement of the firm of which he was boss. His relationship with his children was summed up by the words: "A family that has fun; living, laughing and learning for life together." Your mission statement should describe your vision; it will be even better if this guiding principle radiates a kind of motivating power. There is a difference between the statements "I commit myself to maintaining my marriage" and "I treat my partner as if I had just fallen in love with him/her."

Is there a key phrase that sums up everything in your life? What would you like to be written on your gravestone? In case the cemetery seems too far away, what would you consider to be important if you only had six months to live? Go through your wishes, dreams and visions again. What is the main one? What would you most like to do? What fills you with passion? If time and money were of no consequence, what would you most love to do? Which of your activities benefits others the most in either the professional or private sphere?

Workshop: My mission – what am I here for?

Write down what you want to bring about or achieve in your life, what useful purpose you would like to serve. Do you wish, as a result of your actions, to leave the world a better, a more worthwhile place than it was when you entered it? Would you like to make a small or large contribution to this: for yourself, for others, for society or for humanity? Think about this carefully and answer the following questions:

1. When I let my mind wander, what is it I see myself enjoying doing most of all?

   _____

   _____

   _____

2. Assuming I could be successful at whatever I do, what would that be?

   _____

   _____

   _____

3. If time and money were of no consequence, what would I most enjoy doing?

   _____

   _____

   _____

4.   Which activities in my professional life are of most use to others?

_____

_____

_____

5.   Which activities in my private life are of most use to others?

_____

_____

_____

A good mission statement has five properties. It should be

• personal
• positive
• written in the present tense
• visualizable
• emotional.

For your mission statement as a manager, the following would not be very effective: "At my place of work nobody, if at all possible, should be overburdened and nobody should be hindered in the performance of his or her work." You can see that this mission statement lacks power. How about the following as an alternative: "I strive every day to ensure that my colleagues perform their work with a smile on their faces and that they are able to exploit their potential in the workplace." The desired elements are all present in this statement "I (personal) strive every day (present tense) to ensure (positive) that my colleagues perform their work with a smile on their faces (visual/emotional) and that they are able to exploit their potential in the workplace." Please understand correctly: by formulating this phrase you will not be turning your department into a collection of happy grinners. Once you have internalized this sentence, however, you will reflect anew each day on how to treat your staff as decently as possible, how to remove obstacles from their way and how to make an active contribution to ensuring that your team enjoys its work.

As you complete the workshop, check that the statements you draft all contain the five elements. You may not succeed in this straightaway. No matter. Your mission statement is something you should hone throughout your life. We know how difficult it is to encapsulate what you want to say in just a few convincing words. The following workshop will merely help to get you started. Over the coming years you will be able to revise your statement(s) repeatedly and you will notice how you are gradually getting closer to what is actually important to you.

Workshop: My personal motto for life

Not everyone succeeds in writing a personal motto for life at his or her first attempt. We have therefore developed a beginner's tool. The result will be a motto for life that resembles an unpolished diamond. With a degree of patience, you will be able to turn it into a glittering gem.

1. What is your most important personal dream? (You identified this on page 129.) Write it in the space provided here:

    This answer forms
    puzzle piece number 1.

2. Here is a list of verbs (please complete):

accept	contribute	work	hold in esteem
confirm	lead	applaud	support
give	amaze	learn	_____
inspire	follow	encourage	_____
achieve	love	help	_____
leave behind	question	attain	_____

The three most powerful, meaningful and appealing verbs for me are:

These verbs form puzzle piece number 2.

3. Which group, community, person or purpose do you live for? Here is another short list to get you thinking and that you can add to:

life	loyalty	freedom	dreams
attitude	possibility	legacy	hope
justice	prosperity	courage	_____
inspiration	development	ambition	_____
contribution	humanity	values	_____
mankind	circle of friends	love	_____

Once again, choose the group, person or purpose that means the most to you:

This will be puzzle piece number 3.

Your motto for life will therefore look like this:

My motto for life is to, [puzzle piece number 1] to [puzzle piece number 2], to [puzzle piece number 2] and to [puzzle piece number 2], in order/for [puzzle piece number 3]

Here are a few examples:

- "My motto for life is to create an environment that is challenging and that encourages growth, to care for and support all the people around me."
- "My motto for life is to bring about innovation, to foster cooperation and to win the trust of all those I serve."
- "My motto in life is to breathe in the sunrise, to leave no stone unturned in my search for the happiness that life has to offer."
- "My motto in life is to uphold, discover and support love, trust and honesty in all my relationships."

Reinvent your life

In the previous chapter we set off in search of our potential, the building material of the future. Now that you have also created your "snapshot of the finish," we are ready to go a step further. In the picture below you will see a landscape that terminates in the

How far along the road through life can you see?
Can you see the seventh horizon?

horizon. The "snapshot of the finish" corresponds to the point where heaven and Earth meet – the horizon. Experience tells us that for most people, this area is lost in fog. The different horizons describe how far we can see. Those with a very limited horizon can see hardly more than a day ahead. Those with more distant horizons can see a week, a month or a year ahead. What we want to do is to help you see as far into the distance as possible.

1st horizon: **the day**   We generally have a firm view of the day ahead. What has to be achieved and taken care of today?

2nd horizon: **the week**   Many people plan on a weekly basis as this gives them a good overview and comprises a complete unit of work and rest.

3rd horizon: **the month**   As a rule, appointments are scheduled for the month ahead, but no goals set.

4th horizon: **the year**   This is actually the ideal planning period but only 3 percent of people set themselves solid goals for the year ahead.

5th horizon: **the seven-year period in which you currently find yourself**   From an earlier chapter you know that life can be divided into seven-year segments. When did the period in which you currently find yourself start? When does it end? How have you named it?

6th horizon: **future periods**   How many more seven-year periods are there likely to be in your life? How would you name these?

7th horizon: **snapshot of the finish (vision)**   What should there be right at the end of your life? Can you describe it emotionally and vividly? What kind of legacy do you wish to leave?

These horizons help us to structure our lives in a self-determined way. The following workshop focuses on the 5th, 6th and 7th horizons.

Workshop: My future life periods

- Mark where you stand today!
- How would you name the period in which you are currently living?
- How would you name the next period?
- How would you name the periods that lie further in the future?

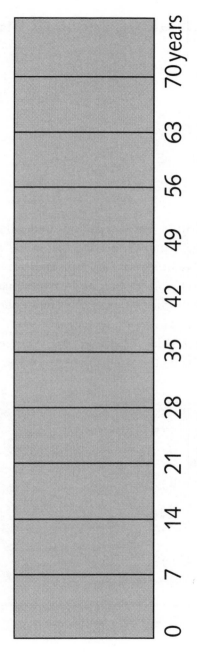

0   7   14   21   28   35   42   49   56   63   70years

Making sense of meaning

If the first half of our lives unfolds under the heading "Striving for success," for many, the second half could be called "Striving for meaning." We don't have to wait until we are in the midst of the midlife crisis before looking at the issues that arise out of it. On the contrary, the earlier we start to examine the question of meaning, the easier it is to overcome this crisis.

In his bestseller *Halftime,* the American entrepreneur Bob Buford describes the two halves of our lives in terms of seven-year periods:

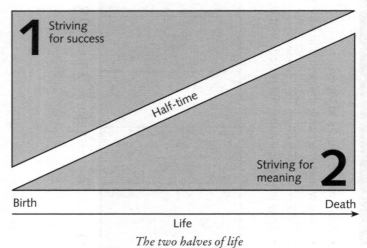

The two halves of life

21–35 years (periods 4 and 5): first half
35–49 years (periods 6 and 7): half-time pause
49–63 years (periods 8 and 9): second half

Unlike a proper soccer match, the first half is governed by different rules to the second. In the first half we are allowed to fall behind. The game is only decided during the second half. It is therefore crucial that we master the rules of the second half.

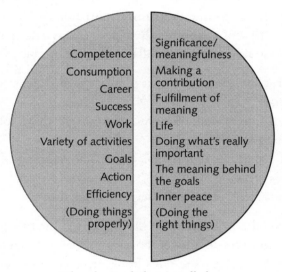

What the two halves are all about

Mankind's key questions

The search for the meaning of life is as old as mankind. Throughout history, our ancestors have asked themselves what they were actually doing on Earth. Mankind's three key questions are:

- Where do I come from?
- Where am I going?
- What is the purpose of life?

In his book *Sophie's World*, Jostein Gaarder sums up the basic questions with which philosophers have occupied (and often tormented) themselves over the millennia as follows:

- How was the world created?
- Is there a will or meaning behind what happens?
- Is there life after death?
- How should we lead our lives?

These are very large questions for a short human life. A German magazine once sent a reporter all over Germany asking people the question: "Could you perhaps tell me what the meaning of life is?"

- Meat products saleswoman Sieglinde replied: "Meaning? What's that then?"
- Musician Oliver said: "The most important thing for me is to stand up to myself."
- Scientific assistant Judith explained: "The meaning of life, OK, listen, it's just kind of…"
- Antje, a student, replied: "To have fun, fun, fun!"

And we could go on and on. One thing is clear: the question of meaning is not easy to answer. For our purposes, however, it is an incredibly important issue. This book promises a self-determined future that can be enjoyed in a state of calm. A life of calm is only conceivable, however, if there is something firm onto which we can hold.

We feel our culture in the third millennium, which is still in its infancy, is neglecting the search for meaning. Before, everything was simpler: institutions such as the church and the state set out the meaning of life and the meaning of our actions. Authorities such as these were barely questioned. People of today, however, see themselves as autonomous. We no longer accept the imposition of meaning from the outside and therefore have to embark on a search for the meaning of existence for ourselves.

In our modern industrial society, little importance is attached to this search for meaning. Over the past few decades, materialism has gained the upper hand. In our materialistic society, meaning has come to be expressed in terms of the size of our monthly pay packet, the number of holidays we have each year, the size of our houses. This purely materialistic meaning can sustain people for many years, but it will sustain practically no one for their whole lives. Most people want to do something meaningful, something that makes sense above and beyond profit margins.

We have to recognize once more that meaning is one of the strongest motivating factors there is. It is the motor that continually gets us moving and gives our lives dynamism. Those who see meaning in what they do are capable of almost anything. Overtime, extra shifts, exceptional effort and many sacrifices – none of this is a problem for those who know why it is worthwhile delivering this level of performance.

Workshop: The quest for meaning

"The third millennium has begun with the realization that people have a right to meaning in their lives. Meaning is a human right," says Gertrud Höhler. What does meaning mean for you?

My view:

- ☐ Life is meaningless
- ☐ The meaning of life is pre-determined
- ☐ I have to define the meaning of life for myself
- ☐ _____

Reasons:

_____

_____

_____

What gives my life meaning?

_____

_____

_____

Why then is the question of meaning so important?

It preoccupies us so because we find it difficult to live on this Earth without any meaning at all in our lives. Those who want to lead a meaningful life must first be clear about what they mean by "life" for we only have one. Everything else can be repeated. If we fail our exams we can resit them, if our marriage breaks down we can have another go with a different partner. Only when we have to reproach ourselves at the end of our lives with "not having taken ourselves seriously" is there no second chance.

A quotation from an unknown source goes:

> The meaning of life lies in doing meaningful things. What is meant by meaningful here is an activity that is of benefit to ourselves, to others and ideally to all of humanity. The meaning of life thus lies in doing useful things, bringing added value to the lives of as many people as possible and in doing good.

Alfred Adler, the founder of Individual Psychology, uses an apposite image for this:

> It is only possible to achieve self-fulfillment by forgetting ourselves, looking beyond ourselves. Is this not like the eye, whose ability to see depends on not seeing itself? When does the eye see anything of itself? Only when it is diseased. If I have cataracts I see a gray cloud which makes me aware of my condition. If I am suffering from glaucoma I see a ring of

> rainbow colors around the light source. This is my 'Green Star'.
> But this also means the ability of my eye to see the world
> around me is diminished and impaired.

Only those who forget themselves and are no longer aware of themselves are clearly proceeding in the right direction.

We realize we are asking a lot of you at this point, but now it is your turn. What are your personal thoughts about the meaning of your life? The reason the answer is so important is that it forms the basis on which you will build your life. People become depressed, unenthusiastic and unwell when they can no longer discern any meaning in their lives. If they rediscover this meaning, they become healthy again overnight.

The extent to which the setting of goals and burning of energy is automatically accompanied by meaninglessness is frightening. The consequences of this are: a lack of joy, little lasting benefit, endogenous neuroses, consumption of alcohol to numb the senses... Meaninglessness blocks energy, meaningfulness unleashes energy.

As he lay on his deathbed, King Henry VIII of England summoned his fool. "I have to go now, my friend" said the king. "Where to?" asked the jester. "I know not." – "When will you return?" – "I shall not return." – "Who will accompany you?" – "No one." – "Have you prepared, then, for this journey?" – "No." – At this the fool took his scepter and cap and threw them onto the king's bed, declaring: "Your Majesty once told me I should give my scepter to any man that is a greater fool than I. You are that man, for you are going you know not where and with no escort."

In the work of Viktor Frankl we read that only when people discover a meaning that reaches beyond their immediate lives can they be said to have found true, sustainable meaning. Psychologist Mihaly Csikszentmihalyi, whose "flow" concept has played a pioneering role in the field of happiness research, explains that coming up with an answer to the question of meaning plays a decisive role in making us happy in every sphere of life because finding meaning in life creates harmony in our consciousness. "The feelings, thoughts and actions of people who have identified their desires and who work meaningfully toward fulfilling them are in accord with each other and an inner harmony is thus achieved." Social philosopher Hannah Arendt goes a stage further. In her view, a superficial desire for a nice life is not enough to endow our lives with meaning. For this we need "ultimate goals" – goals that extend beyond the grave.

How do we find this meaning? Those who do not set out in search of it will never find it. We do not have to reinvent the wheel in our intimate search for the meaning of life – even if we were convinced there was nothing we could learn from anyone else in this area. Mihaly Csikszentmihalyi gets to the heart of this in the following:

> To disregard the information gathered in difficult circumstances by our ancestors on how to lead one's life, or to expect to be able to invent a viable system of goals all by ourselves, is misguided arrogance. Our chances of success are as small as they would be if we were to try to build an electron microscope without either the necessary tools or any knowledge of physics.

We recommend that you devote time to this question of meaning and to studying what has given meaning to the lives of successful historical and contemporary figures. What is it that has driven inventors and discoverers, reformers and social revolutionaries, artists and top managers to achieve great things? Do not exclude religion from your research. Many people from all sections of society have only found adequate meaning in life once they have come to see themselves as part of God's creation.

While it is considered perfectly normal in the US to conduct a search for meaning of this kind in the churches, in Germany the question of religion has an alienating effect on many people. A new trend has recently been observed, however. The Institute for Demoscopy in Allensbach discovered in 2002 that around 70 percent of top businessmen describe themselves as religious, a dramatic increase over the previous ten years.

When you have found a meaning, not only will this unleash new feelings of happiness inside you, it will also enable you to cope far better with crises and difficult strokes of fate. One of the most astonishing examples of this is English astrophysicist Stephen Hawking. This famous scientist and bestselling author (*A Brief History of Time*) contracted motor neurone disease, which is incurable and affects the brain, spinal cord and muscles, in childhood. His doctors gave Hawking until the age of 22 to live. He can barely move or speak. He can give lectures only with the assistance of a speech synthesizer. On January 8, 2002 he celebrated his 60th birthday. Hawking has dedicated his (physically handicapped) life to astrophysics and the linking of relativity theory to quantum mechanics. He is regarded by many as a second Einstein.

Does Hawking moan about the unimaginable and dramatic limitations that his illness has imposed on him? On the contrary, he makes jokes about it, claiming that as a result of having to spend his life in a wheelchair, at least he has not had the temptation to fritter away his time jogging or playing golf. He also talks in all seriousness of having had enjoyed "great fortune" in life, privately as well as professionally. In an interview he declared that the illness had not been that big a blow. "Before I found life rather boring. I think I'm happier now."

Stephen Hawking has found meaning in his research, in getting to the bottom of life's unsolved problems. Where would the meaning of your life lie if for some reason you could no longer drive to work every day? The path towards meaning is arduous but crucial. The knowledge of what you are here for and why you do what you do will release new strength within you. If, on the other hand, you are not convinced that your commitment to your family, friends and company makes a difference, you will soon get frustrated. This can even be measured. Since 1972, the Allensbach opinion researchers have repeatedly demonstrated that an extremely close relationship exists between the subjective feeling of being able to make a meaningful contribution at work and the quality of our work, our sickness levels and our willingness to help our colleagues. This is true at all levels, from factory floor to boardroom.

It is quite clear that the search for the meaning of our own existence and behavior is worth the effort it involves. If you know the reasons why you *should* do something, you will also *want* to do it. Meaning sets things in motion. Have you discovered the meaning of your life?

Third step:
Implement offensively

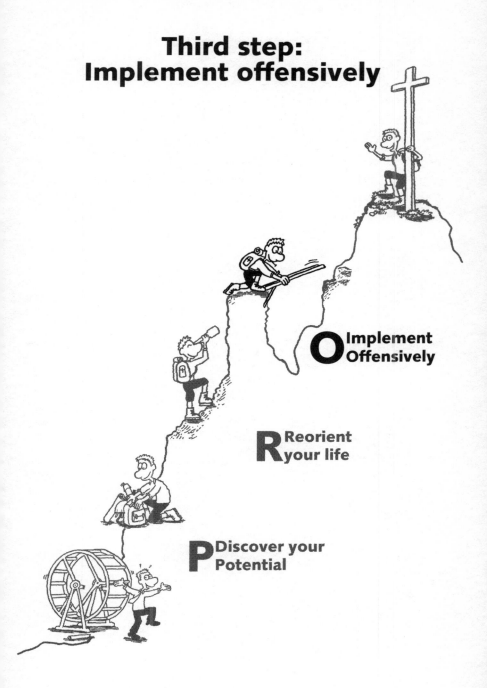

O Implement
Offensively

R Reorient
your life

P Discover your
Potential

Someone who does something is more successful than someone
who knows of a thousand things that ought to be done

Proverb

You will certainly be familiar with proverbs like "The road to Hell
is paved with good intentions" and "Procrastination is the thief of
time." We know a great deal, a very great deal, but how much of it
do we put into practice? There has never been more theoretical
know-how; there have never been so many books and self-help
materials. But what will actually push us into taking action and
changing our lives?

One day, a manager invited me into his office, closed the door
and took a piece of paper out of his drawer, unfolding it with great
pride. He had sketched out a vision for himself and a perfect plan of
how to realize it. But his plan had been lying in that drawer for at
least two years without being worked on. No one except him knew
about this piece of paper, and he had not yet put any of it into
practice. As the manager said, "Everyday life is so demanding and
full, there's no time left over to think about implementing it." As
the consultation process continued, it became clear that his plan
really was a brilliant one. But it had very nearly remained no more
than a pipe dream.

A person of average gifts will be far superior to an inconsistent
genius when it comes to implementing plans systematically. I have
often been saddened and shocked to meet highly gifted people who
simply "didn't have their feet on the ground." In the previous

chapter, you will have developed a vision covering various areas of your life. But how can what you have learned be put into practice in the real world? According to a Chinese saying, "A man must keep his mouth open a long while before a roast pigeon flies into it."

As important as it is to have a vision that gives your life direction, this vision needs to be in touch with everyday life if it is to be more than just a dream. Imagine a farmer who has an exact understanding of the qualities of the soil in his fields and uses this knowledge to draw up a brilliant plan setting out which crops he will plant when and where. But what is the use of the best soil in the world if he just sits and dreams in his living room? The farmer will only profit from it if he rolls up his shirtsleeves and sets to work. What would have become of Mother Teresa if she had merely dreamed of helping the poor and desperate? There are plenty of books by good dreamers. Our world needs people who get things done.

Your vision will give you direction, but you will have to break this model down into realistic short-term and medium-term steps. There are people who fervently love to dream, but who hate getting down to the nitty-gritty. By the same token, there are practical types who prefer to occupy themselves with everyday trivia rather than thinking about why they are doing something and what their goal actually is. Both vision and action are important! Only a combination of vision and the determination to act will lead you to your goal.

The steps suggested in this chapter will prevent you getting bogged down in theorizing and help you reap the blessings of a proactive way of life in the here and now. It is not the person who knows a thousand things, but the person who makes the right move who will come closer to his or her goal.

How to turn your wishes into goals

The Californian coast lay shrouded in fog on the morning of July 4, 1952. On Catalina Island, 21 miles to the west, a 34-year-old woman was wading into the water and setting out to swim towards California – determined to be the first woman swimmer to make it to the mainland. The water was freezing and the fog was so thick she could hardly make out the support boats.

Millions watched her on national television. Several times, sharks had to be driven away with rifles to protect the lonely figure. Tiredness was never a great problem for her on long-distance swims of this kind – it was the icy cold that made her struggle. More than 15 hours later, she begged, frozen stiff, to be lifted out of the water. She could go on no further. Her mother and her trainer, who were traveling in the boat next to her, told her she was very close to the shore. They urged her not to give up, but as she looked across towards the Californian coastline she saw nothing but thick fog and repeated her request to be pulled out of the water.

Hours later, once her body had thawed out, she was hit by the shock of her failure. She had given up just short of her goal, only half a mile from the coast! A reporter asked her what had stopped her from swimming the last half-mile. She said that the fog was to blame, and that if only she could have seen the shore she could have made it! The problem was that while she was swimming out there she could not see her goal. Two months later, Florence Chadwick made a second attempt at swimming the Catalina Channel. Although it was foggy again, she reached the mainland – she had her sights set firmly on her goal!

Goals are a simple yet exceedingly powerful tool. For the most part, we use them and benefit from their positive effects without really being aware of what we are doing. They are essential if our lives are to move in the right direction.

If you do not know where you want to go, you cannot really make any plans. Aimlessness usually results in a failure to plan, or unproductive activity undertaken for its own sake. I know what I am talking about because I myself lived in this trap for years. You may feel important and often beaver away doing a great deal of work, but nothing really changes for the better. However, a plan will help you to tell whether you are making progress and judge how far you have got. Without a plan, you cannot expect to know what it feels like to enjoy success and will lack any "conscious

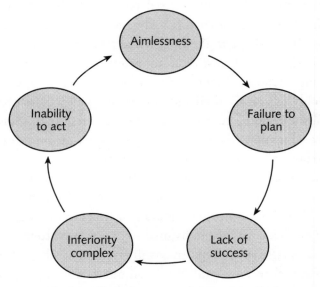

Neglect of basic human needs (negative spiral)

experience of progress." This causes frustration – "I work like a dog, but somehow I am always going round in circles" – strengthening inferiority complexes and other negative feelings that result in demotivation and a further inability to act. What a depressing cycle!

Imagine you get onto a bus that is going to take you somewhere. Maybe you simply find it calming to be sitting in a moving bus. But after you have driven past the place where you boarded it for the tenth time, you notice that the bus keeps going round in circles. Do you find this satisfying? People who lack peace and balance tend to put a positive gloss on times like this. At least something is happening. It feels so good to be sitting in a bus at last, relaxing and not having to do anything. Maybe the bus you are sitting in is not even going round in circles, but keeps driving in the wrong direction – a direction that may be right for other people, but not for you. At some point, you suddenly realize there is a danger you may not catch your connection. Then you start to panic – or resign yourself to the situation.

There is always hope, but only if you get off that bus. In most cases, the longer you wait before taking your life in hand and acting purposefully to shape it, the further the way back will be and the more energy it will cost you to reach *your* goal in spite of everything. Choose your destination and plan your route accordingly. If you are tired and burned out, you will be better off consciously deciding to recharge your batteries. Take some time out to build up new reserves of energy, but only get on a bus if it is going to take you closer to where *you* want to be.

Clear, appropriate goals will help you make plans and succeed in achieving your ambitions. Anyone who knows where they want to go can think about how they should be getting there. A good plan allows you to identify the individual steps you need to take. If you can manage these small steps, they will give you a feeling of success and so strengthen your confidence and motivation. These, in turn, will be sources of energy for the next stage of your journey.

Why don't you give it a try? Make up your mind to clear out a particular room (your office, your bedroom, the garage...). Draw up a realistic plan of attack, and break up the task into meaningful steps: first the shelves, then the cupboards, then the floor... Each step you complete will give you a sense of success, a feeling that will motivate you and lead you to your goal.

Consideration of basic human needs (positive spiral)

What makes good goals

One goal is not as good as another. Setting goals is an art that has to be learned. It is like any other tool: the more skillfully you can handle it, the better the results. Practice makes perfect. You do not throw away a hammer just because it bruises your thumb the first time you bang in a nail. It was not the hammer's fault; nor are you simply "too stupid" to use a hammer. It was simply lack of experience. And practice makes perfect!

The three M-criteria are a very simple way of reminding yourself what sort of goals you should be pursuing. Goals must be:

- measurable
- manageable
- motivating.

These minimum requirements have helped many people to set good goals in the past.

Measurable goals

Is it possible to measure whether you have reached a goal? The worst enemies of achievable goals are vague, general declarations of intent. You want to do something, sometime, somehow. But how are you going to set about it?

One thing people often say is, "I really want to spend more time with my family." Is this a goal? No! Why not? Because the words "more time" do not relate to anything that can be measured. When will you have achieved this goal? Do you want to spend two days a week with your family? Or were you thinking of Friday evenings? Or a holiday together? You will have gathered that this way of expressing what you want to do is not precise enough. However, if you do not wish to tie yourself down, there is a danger that you will not know when and how you should address the issue or even recognize when you have finally achieved your goal.

Let us assume that one part of your vision is a fulfilled family life. You intend to strengthen the bonds that hold your family together. You might set yourself an achievable goal such as: "I will deliberately leave the television switched off after supper during the week and spend half an hour listening to and understanding what my partner and children have to say." Putting it in these terms enables you to judge quite clearly afterwards whether you have achieved the goal or not. Of course, the idea is not to measure your half-hours precisely down to the last second with a stopwatch. But your intention has been framed in clear, precise and measurable terms.

Another example: You urgently need to improve your Spanish skills for work. Is this a goal? No. Because, again, it is not expressed precisely enough. It would be a goal if you decided to take two hours every Monday evening to work through a chapter of your *Business Spanish* book. What is more, there is no reason why you should not reward yourself with a portion of your favorite ice cream at the end of each chapter!

Goals focus our efforts and release energy. But if they are to do this, they must be clear and unambiguous. Imagine you are full of energy but do not know what you should do with it. The clearer and more focused your approach, the more energy will be channeled into achieving your goal rather than frittered away trying to answer the question "What could I be doing?" Targeted planning followed up by targeted implementation is the key to success. If you can exploit the dynamic described above, you will rediscover how good it feels to keep on developing yourself.

Manageable goals

What is the use of the best measurable goals if they are impossible to achieve? Or if you are pursuing too many of them at the same time?

Sometimes we simply aim too high, and this is also frustrating over the long term. I encounter this regularly in the sales departments of certain companies where the goals set are based on ludicrously optimistic figures. People must have a realistic chance of achieving their goals. A short while ago, we advised a company where dramatically unrealistic goals were being set. When we discussed the issue, the manager responsible justified it by saying that he needed exaggerated goals of this kind so that his staff made some kind of effort in the first place. He had sensed something correct, but still made a great mistake. We humans need goals that are demanding and challenging, but making excessive demands is a pathologically misguided way of tapping into this dynamic.

You should always seek the healthiest way of doing things over the long term. You need to approach life like a long-distance runner, not a sprinter. However necessary it may be to drive at high speed for a while at times, it will have destructive consequences if you constantly keep the accelerator pressed to the floor. In some ways, working out where this healthy mean lies and following it through life is a question of maturity. We want to "do a lot" with our lives, which means our goals have to be challenging, but they should not overwhelm us. The dividing line is narrow, but distinct.

Another company's engineers were given an assignment that was supposed to have been finished "the day before yesterday." This deadline had deliberately been manipulated as a way of pushing them to work as hard as they possibly could. Everyone secretly expected the assignment to take two weeks, both the manager in charge and his staff. In consequence, all the deadlines given in the files were wrong. However, this was just part of the rules of the game in that company. Internally, there was a second plan with the real schedule that was never set down in writing. Everyone knew this and worked according to it, even though the unrealistic deadline was always quoted orally and in writing. The whole situation changed abruptly when a competitor who set realistic deadlines tried to poach staff and clients.

Think about your own plans. Are they manageable? Or would the commitments you have made fill 25 hours a day? In time-management seminars, we always ask the participants to list what they have decided to do the following day. Mostly, the result is a wonderful list of sensible, practical, useful tasks. The next step is to get the participants to estimate how long it will take to complete each task (at first without including the buffer times that would actually be required). Then we ask them to add up how long would be needed for all the jobs they want to do the next day. It is sometimes shocking how unrealistic these plans can be, even those drawn up by people who otherwise possess a great deal of wisdom. Many have learned nothing from their experiences over the years, but still go home frustrated every evening: "I didn't get everything important done again today!"

What you have decided to do must therefore be manageable for you – every single task and all of them taken together! Your goals can be ambitious – a challenge is good for us – but you should not have too many of them. One small warning: In the last few years, we have had the opportunity to assist numerous companies making the transition to management systems based on the agreement of goals. If you set goals for others, it is absolutely essential that you listen to your staff, otherwise you will get caught in the same trap over and over again. Many processes of this kind have failed or resulted in output levels lagging far behind potential because, in fact, *goals have been imposed* rather than *agreed*. Agreement means that both sides have to genuinely accept the goals that are being set.

Motivating goals

The third important point is one that, unfortunately, people often lose sight of: Do you find the goal you want to achieve motivating? In most cases, goals that do little or nothing to motivate you are just as unsuitable as unclear, unrealistic intentions.

In the first chapter of this book, we described what motivates people: the avoidance of pain and enjoyment of pleasure. If you take these motivational factors into account, you will reach your goals more easily. The goal of cutting your weight by 10 pounds over the next month is measurable and (if you are pretty hard on yourself) manageable as well. However, it is not the bare figures that give this goal its motivational power, but the feelings you associate with the result. Think about it visually: the pretty evening

dress you bought the year before last will fit again; jogging will not wear you out so much any more (and your joints will also suffer less stress once you have lost weight); if you reduce the amount of food you eat, you will be able to think more clearly and work more effectively again. You can already feel what you are working towards. In future, a slimmer waistline will make you feel more attractive, sportier and more energetic. On its own, the clear idea of a result that appeals to your emotional world will help you to say no to the temptations of chocolate at crucial moments.

And now a quick test. Please tick which of the following statements are goals of the kind discussed above and which are, at best, wishes or declarations of intent.

Test: Wish or goal?

Please tick the correct boxes:

Wish or goal?	Goal	Wish
1. I want to become a better father/mother.	☐	☐
2. I want to order information material on professional development opportunities by the end of the quarter.	☐	☐

3. From now on, I will conduct staff appraisal interviews. ☐ ☐

4. I will have the sales figures for the previous week presented to me on a regular basis. ☐ ☐

5. As of next week, I will begin my working day with a "quiet hour" at 8.00 a.m. on Tuesdays and Thursdays. ☐ ☐

6. I will exercise regularly. ☐ ☐

Solution:
Statements 1, 3 and 6 are wishes. Statements 2, 4 and 5 are real goals.

Our company in the US is based on the Mississippi, a broad, powerful river. Crossing it is quite a challenge. When you set off in a boat heading for a point exactly opposite on the other bank, you can find yourself being carried off for miles downstream by the current and end up further from your goal than ever before. Does this mean your goal was wrong? No – you may just have to take a boat with a more powerful engine or first steer some way upstream in order to land at the right point. And if you start in the morning fog, there is always a chance that you will land on one of the islands instead of the other side of the river. Setting goals often means managing discrepancies.

Maybe you are still unsure about how to formulate "real" goals that meet the criteria explained above. If so, look at the following examples before writing up your own goals in the next workshop.

- Wish: I would like to lose weight.
  Goal: I will jog for half an hour every day and stop eating chocolate.
- Wish: I want to be a good father to my daughter.
  Goal: I will reserve 15 minutes every day when I will concentrate on talking to her and listening carefully to what she has to say.

Apart from this, I will invest at least an hour every week in spending time just with her; playing cards, going to the cinema, eating ice cream etc.

- Wish: I do not want to end up at a loose end once my professional career is over.

  Goal: I will act today and draw up a plan setting out realistically how I will spend the first year after I retire. This plan will include voluntary work, adult education courses, visits, days spent decorating the house etc. for each month.

- Wish: I would like to do more for my professional development.

  Goal: I will obtain a brochure from the local adult education college and sign up for a class this month.

Workshop: Turning your wishes into goals

Now it is your turn. You analyzed your wishes in the workshop on pages 125–129 so use your results to formulate measurable, manageable, motivating goals. You will need to use this "art" again and again if you want to plan your life and career successfully. It will be one of your main tasks on your dream day to break down dreams into achievable goals.

1. Wish
   Goal: _____
   Goal: _____
   Goal: _____

2. Wish
   Goal: _____
   Goal: _____
   Goal: _____

3. Wish
   Goal: _____
   Goal: _____
   Goal: _____

From the urgent to the important

If you think about all the things you could, should and have to do, you will probably end up with a very long list. It would be nice to be able to do all of them, but it is impossible to put so many plans into practice.

Imagine you have a bottle of fine Italian wine and two brandy glasses. How will you fit the entire contents of the bottle into the two glasses without drinking any of the wine, spilling it, allowing it to evaporate or freezing it?

Do you have a solution? Remember your physics lessons at school! Of course, it will not work. It is just as impossible for you to cope with every job to be dealt with immediately yourself. The two glasses could stand symbolically for the morning and the afternoon. What is stopping you from simply taking a third glass and making plans for the evening as well? You will be amazed: most times when someone tries this, another full bottle suddenly appears, demanding to be fitted in as well.

I was told by a contemporary that he regularly lists everything that he should, must and could do. Once he has drawn up his list, he sits in front of it feeling a mixture of enthusiasm and exhaustion. Where should he begin? Prioritization is the magic word in this situation! Imagine you are standing on your balcony and contemplating with satisfaction what you have earned that day, three banknotes worth 500, 50 and 5 dollars. Suddenly, you are surprised by an unexpected gust of wind that rips all three notes from your hand and sends them racing towards the edge of the balcony. Which note will you try to grab first? A stupid question really: it has to be the most valuable one!

Talking about time management, Stephen R. Covey puts forward the pebble principle. He describes time as a jar that has to be filled with stones, sand and water. The first step is to put the big stones – your most important priorities – into the jug. These are the essential components of a responsible life. Once the stones are in the jar, you can fill up the remaining space with less important things, such as small pebbles, sand and water.

If you start with the sand when you begin filling up your jar, it will probably be full before you can put in the first stone. If you have a great deal to do, you should not simply set about it at random. Think for a moment: What are your biggest, most valuable, most difficult jobs? These are, to stay with the image, your "pebbles."

Weekly, monthly and yearly plans based on the pebble principle that define priorities and reserve time windows for what is really important are the keys to harmonious time management and life balance. If you have not just decided in your own mind what is important, but also set it down in writing, you will find it considerably easier to say no to activities that are urgent but unimportant – and yes to activities that will take you closer to your life goals.

The unpredictable nature of everyday working life means that if you do not do this something else will always get in the way sooner or later – and you will quickly find your diary filling up with activity after activity all by itself. What is important will be left by the wayside while you attend to urgent matters.

Of important and urgent tasks

Is it difficult to distinguish urgent from important tasks? Yes, it is difficult. But if you can master this distinction, it will enable you to manage your time with a completely new sense of independence. Just try it out:

Test: Important or urgent?

1. Your car is supposed to be serviced every 15,000 miles. According to the milometer, another service is due next week.
   ☐ Urgent   ☐ Important
2. You realize in the evening that you have still not read your daily newspaper.
   ☐ Urgent   ☐ Important
3. The new year has begun, but you have still not given any thought to your goals for the year.
   ☐ Urgent   ☐ Important
4. You like to go to the dentist twice a year for a checkup. It is the autumn and your teeth are not causing you any trouble, but you have not yet been to see the dentist this year.
   ☐ Urgent   ☐ Important

(Solution: 1. Important, not urgent, because it does not require your immediate attention; your car can still do a few hundred miles without a service. 2. Urgent, not important, because reading the daily newspaper will not take you any closer to your goals. 3. Important and possibly urgent; not having any goals will not necessarily have any direct impact on your work; but it would become urgent if your bank asked to see your business goals before extending your credit line. 4. Important, not urgent.)

Urgent tasks make us feel they have to be dealt with immediately, but they are not automatically important. They make us feel: This needs my immediate attention – now! You will recognize important tasks because they take you closer to your goals.

One good example of something that creates an impression of urgency is the telephone. If a mobile phone rings somewhere in a train, lots of people are startled and reach for their own phones, like cowboys reaching instinctively for their Colts. Telephone calls tend to be treated as matters of vital importance. Do you stay calm when your telephone rings or do you start as well? "Hello, Meyers here. No, sorry, wrong number. No problem, bye." Was it important? No, just urgent...

By contrast, important tasks take you closer to your central personal and professional goals. Is it important to make sure you exercise properly? At first it may not seem to matter much. You get by perfectly well without it. But as the saying goes, "Those who do not take time for exercise will have to reserve time for sickness."

US President Eisenhower used to divide up what he had to do between four squares:

- Tasks that are important and urgent (Square 1)
- Tasks that are important (Square 2)
- Tasks that are urgent (Square 3)
- Tasks that are neither important nor urgent (Square 4)

Assess yourself: What percentage of your time do you spend on each square? If you like, you can also write in how much of your time you feel you ought to be spending on each of them. Below, you will find a list of typical activities for the different squares that will help you fill in your answers.

The more time you spend on urgent tasks, the higher your adrenaline level will rise. This is usually associated with rushing, stress and last-minute solutions. People can cope with this kind of pace for a while, but nobody can keep it up over the long term. We have also summarized the typical results of spending a great deal of time on each of the squares.

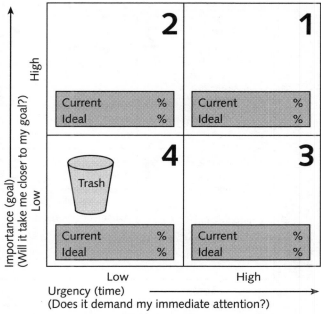

Distinguishing the important from the urgent

The positive things that happen when you take time for Square 2 activities are quite astounding. Typically, managers invest 10 to 30 percent of their time in this square. It should be very clear that if you just reduce how long you spend on the other three squares by a few percentage points and invest the time this sets free in Square 2, your life will change dramatically!

I know two managers, one of them hectic, bad-tempered, always working flat out. In fact, he lives on the brink of burnout and regularly needs psychiatric drugs. His life is like one long emergency. Everything seems to be a matter of life and death. He works day and night. His marriage exists only on paper.

His colleague has a job in the same industry and is about the same age, has the same number of staff under him, works on the same product and puts in an average of 50 hours a week. But he radiates calm, balance, thoughtfulness and concentration. He still

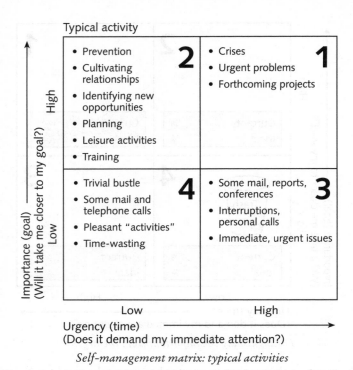

Self-management matrix: typical activities

notices little things, such as a staff member's new haircut, and always has time for a quick chat with his neighbor.

When you get to know both of them, you notice that the second manager is often able to concentrate hard on Square 2 activities. He does a great deal of intensive planning and develops his staff with long-term aims in view, while the other, due to pressure of time, demotivates his staff by treating them as mere recipients of orders.

Each important task that you do not address will inevitably become "urgent and important" (Square 1 task). A significant member of staff who is not given the attention he needs will leave the firm. At the same time, another important problem will crop up: deciding who should succeed him.

Square 2 activities have one thing in common: At first, nothing happens if you do not pay them any attention. This is deceptive. If

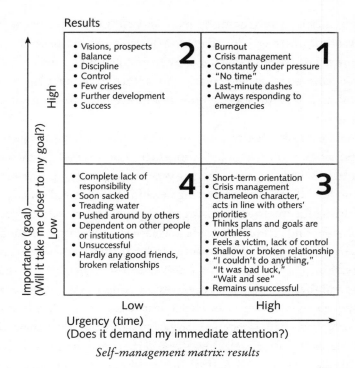

Results

Self-management matrix: results

you do not eat properly or look after your physical fitness, you will not drop dead straightaway as a result. But, over the long term, you will be ill more often and will be less resilient. Maybe you are not planning your next career move? You probably still have plenty to do and, at most, will wonder why younger colleagues keep getting promoted past you ever more rapidly. In theory, career planning is not terribly urgent – but it can be incredibly important.

First of all, allocate the things you do to the relevant squares. Tasks that are important and urgent can be designated as Square 1 tasks and enjoy the highest priority. You should deal with these tasks immediately yourself.

You should regularly plan in plenty of time for Square 2 tasks. This will protect you from massive stress. For example, set up a system you can use to keep track of your finances before the bank has to impose a restructuring plan on you. Or always work from your home office on Thursdays so you can concentrate on the most important questions you face away from the frantic rush of day-to-day events at your workplace. An annual training plan is very useful as a way of approaching tasks that have to be dealt with repeatedly.

Square 3 tasks that are only urgent should be delegated as much as possible, if not avoided altogether. For example, you could regularly schedule periods when you are undisturbed, leaving any telephone calls to your answering machine for a limited time.

Surfing the internet, choosing promotional gifts, leafing through catalogues and interesting trade magazines – these typical Square 4 tasks do not exert any pressure. Indeed, they can be a form of relaxation. I have observed a number of top managers for several days and they all appeared very busy and important, whatever they happened to be doing. On closer inspection, it was evident how cleverly they had integrated Square 4 activities into their daily routine as a way of relaxing. To a certain extent, such activities should be a controlled part of our working day. We suggest that you consciously plan a maximum of 10 percent of your time for activities of this kind, but do not exceed this limit.

And now a question. Which square is responsible for your successes in life? Correct, it is Square 2. This is why you should work on a long-term Square 2 task every day. Apart from your daily business, you must also think about "strategically" important tasks and goals. Only then will what you do today make you a success tomorrow

Workshop: Saying no

Accept that you will never have enough time to do all the things you could do and that other people would like you to do. Make sure you use your time to do what is most important to you and takes you closer to your aims. You can only gain the time to do this by saying no to the less important things and not getting involved in them.

Saying no: In future, I intend to say no to the following inquiries, tasks or expectations in order to concentrate on my own values and goals again:

1. _____
2. _____
3. _____
4. _____
5. _____

Throwing away: I intend to throw away the following objects over the next few days in order to make space in my surroundings again so I can work on my real goals:

1. _____
2. _____
3. _____
4. _____
5. _____

The Pareto Principle – "80/20 Rule"

There is another principle you should certainly not ignore in your planning: the Pareto Principle. The 19th-century economist Vilfredo Pareto studied, among other things, questions of income and property distribution, and made a discovery that he found highly significant: a recurrent mathematical relationship between the size of a group (as a percentage of the entire relevant population) and its level of income or assets. In this context, the exact proportions are less important than the fact that the distribution of assets within the population was predictably unbalanced. He called this the 80/20 rule.

This rule describes an imbalance between causes and effects, expenditure and profit, activities and results. A typical distributional pattern shows that 80 percent of profit derives from 20 percent of expenditure, 80 percent of effects are determined by 20 percent of causes and 80 percent of results are achieved by 20 percent of activities.

You are probably familiar with the problem: You urgently have to put together an invitation to your company's anniversary celebrations. It does not take you long to compose the text and complete 80 percent of the work. But then you begin to polish what you have written and decide to quickly scan a picture and insert it. Suddenly, you find you have spent dramatically more time on the last 20 percent of the work than on the first 80 percent.

Further examples (which have not been calculated precisely down to the last percentage point – it is the general proportions that matter):

- 20 percent of products generate 80 percent of turnover
- 20 percent of clients bring in 80 percent of turnover
- 20 percent of offenders cause 80 percent of all criminal damage
- 20 percent of drivers are responsible for 80 percent of accidents
- 20 percent of a carpet suffers 80 percent of the wear and tear

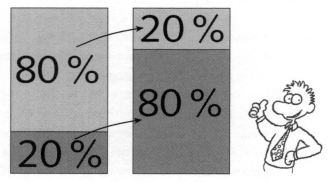

What is important? What is unimportant?

- We wear 20 percent of our clothes 80 percent of the time
- 20 percent of possible causes trigger 80 percent of false alarms
- 20 percent of churchgoers give 80 percent of donations
- 20 percent of staff take 80 percent of sick days
- 20 percent of teachers give 80 percent of homework.

It will be evident that some of the things we do are many more times productive than the others. What does this mean for us and our daily routine? It means, for example, that 15 minutes invested in a member of staff may help them to work more successfully and effectively. Who are your most important clients? Who are your most important suppliers? How can you improve your relationships with them? You cannot always do everything, so concentrate on the 20 percent of your work that guarantees 80 percent of your success!

Would it not be better to go for an 80 percent solution (making a relatively small investment) than drop a project because 100 percent is unattainable anyway? Hopefully, this idea will give you the courage to cast light into a few of the "dark corners" of your working life and relationships.

This highlights yet again the great difference between efficiency and effectiveness. Remember, efficiency means doing things right, effectiveness means doing the right things. You will save a great deal of time and energy if you focus on effectiveness instead of efficiency. Leading managers in the business world have confirmed the truth of this principle. Surgeons, dentists and parents also say the Pareto rule has helped them to work more successfully (although, to be honest, we find it a little scary to hear this from the surgeons). What are the activities that produce 80 percent of the results for you? You need to identify them and deal with them first.

Central areas of your life – your main tasks

Have you ever bothered to draw up an overview of all the commitments you are tangled up in? Where have you taken on responsibilities? What obligations are you under? For some people, this is a very simple exercise. By contrast, others list up to 30 key responsibilities. It is interesting that these are usually the people who groan more or less loudly about having too much to do. I know a mother of five children who is politically active, sitting on the council of the small town where she lives. In addition to this, she has a responsible position on the parish committee and runs a charitable organization that does a great deal of campaigning for poor countries. Furthermore, she is a keen artist, looks after a big house and owns lots of pets. This woman copes amazingly well with her daily life. But she is the exception. Most people get bogged down, lose track of what they are doing and can hardly begin to deliver on the promises they make to others.

The technique described below will help you to keep track of what you have to do. Just writing out all the activities I am committed to shocked me and made me more responsible about taking on new tasks.

We would like you to draw up a mindmap. This is like a sketch map of your priorities and can be a great help when you want to order your thoughts. Write a topic in the middle, as in the example on page 187, where we have chosen "My life (areas of responsibility)." Next, write down your key areas of responsibility branching out from it: in this case "Me," Work, Household duties, Marriage/Family, Relationships/Friends and Voluntary work. If your job plays a very central role in your life, you can divide it up into several sub-branches. Maybe you coach managers, provide consultancy services to firms, develop products and run seminars, do research work and have an interest in human resources management.

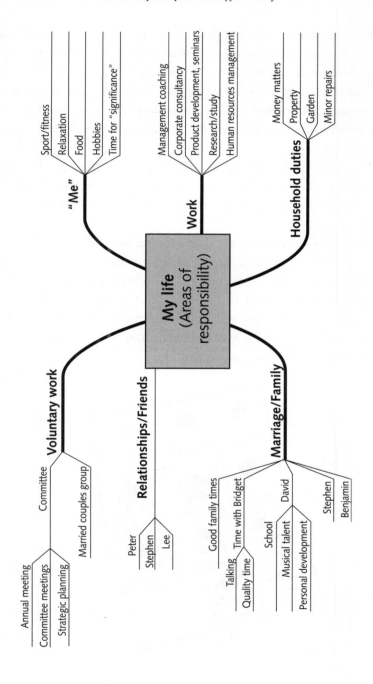

It is up to you how detailed you make your mindmap. I have saved my mindmap on my computer and always add any major new permanent tasks to it. At the beginning, I was not even confident enough to show this diagram to anyone else. But it was a very instructive exercise. I now only accept a new responsibility in the awareness that I will have to cut back on other things to make room for it.

Can you do this? If not, you must learn to say no. It is better to disappoint people straightaway than be constantly dissatisfied for five years because you are unable to do everything you are supposed to be doing.

You come home worn out with a thousand things still to do. You fall into bed exhausted, feeling bad because you ought to have sorted out this, that and the other. As you begin to relax, everything you did not get round to floats to the top of your mind, your adrenaline level rises and you find it impossible to get to sleep. The next morning, the alarm clock rings far too early – here we go all over again... No! Please, not again!

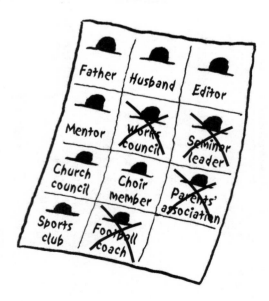

The power of habit

Once we have learned to tell what is urgent from what is important, we should take note of another distinction that is helpful when setting goals: that between one-off goals and habitual goals. One-off goals relate to unique activities that only happen once, habitual goals have to be addressed regularly. If you want to run an orderly office, you should get it thoroughly organized once and for all. We have colleagues who are paid 2,500 dollars a day to help stressed managers tidy up their offices. Once a system has been anchored, you can set yourself the habitual goal of maintaining it. Do not allow yourself to leave work each Friday or – even better – each evening before everything is in its proper place.

Goals are an important aid for all areas of life. Some of us are brilliant at goal-setting in our work, but neglect it in other fields. You need goals for your personal development, your relationships, your family, your exercise routine… Later in this book, we suggest a compact model that will help you in all these areas.

Is it actually possible to set specific goals for phases of your life that are still far off in the future? Of course, the longer the timeframe set for a goal, the greater the need for regular updates and upgrades. Long-term goals have to be regularly revised, cultivated and adjusted.

Why habitual goals are so important

Which trap do you think people get caught in most frequently when they learn new habits? Correct – falling back into their old habits. We humans are creatures of habit, some of us more so than others. Are you aware that you always put your shoes on in the same order? Maybe you always slip into your right slipper first, but pull on your left trainer before the right when you go jogging. Pay attention to this some time. You go through all your morning rituals almost automatically. Waking up, stretching, putting your alarm clock on snooze for another five minutes, getting out of bed, going to the bathroom and making coffee. Then, with the comfortingly warm cup in your hand, you begin your tour round the children's rooms: "Time to get uuuuuuuup!"

Maybe you have different habits, but you will certainly perform rituals that help you cope with the morning, get your working day started and structure your holidays.

Habits are not good or bad in themselves, and it is important to ask yourself whether these habits are good or bad *for you*. You can get used to eating too fast or at a leisurely pace. You can get used to

planning your time or getting stressed around lunch because you still want to end the day successfully after messing about all morning.

Old habits like this die hard, and the only successful strategy for getting rid of bad habits is to replace them with new ones. As a rule, if you practice something for 15 days in a row, you will be well on the way to developing a new habit.

On my dream day, I always think about new habits I would like to learn, what you might call my "annual habit training plan." For example, in order to have more time for my children, I thought of giving each of my three offspring a voucher at the beginning of the month entitling them to two or three hours' activity alone with their dad. No sooner said than done: within the framework of a limited budget, they were able to choose what they wanted to do with their time with me. One of my sons dragged me onto a big trampoline for the first time in my life, the second wanted to eat at a Greek restaurant, the third simply felt like spending some time looking round the shops. Once a month may not seem much, but the more children you have the more challenging this plan will be! Once everyone had got used to it, "Dad's monthly activity voucher" rapidly became a popular institution. My children have been glad to help me make it a new habit, one none of us would want to miss out on. You would be amazed at all the things I have found myself doing in the last year that I would never have considered had it not been for my children. And the activities I have shared with my children have made me terribly aware how selectively I live my life. I fear that a diving course will come up one day. Years ago, this would have filled me with horror, but now I would see it as an opportunity to explore a new world and marvel at the quiet under the water, the amazing colors…

Do you live with a partner? The amount of effort we put into showing our partner that we love them falls off dramatically once we find ourselves in a permanent relationship. It is still important nevertheless. Your relationship is like a bank account; everything that is good for the other partner is a credit paid in, everything else is most probably a debit transaction. What is the balance of your relationship account?

Make a habit of "paying into" your relationship accounts with people who are important to you. This may involve congratulating your staff and giving them presents on their birthdays or conducting regular staff appraisal interviews two or three times a year. I have got into the habit of taking my wife out for a substantial brunch in a nice hotel at the beginning of every month, something she appreciates greatly.

One challenge I face is my habit of giving her a little gift every week: maybe flowers, maybe a magazine, a few nice chocolates or a new CD. You might well be asking yourself why I bother doing this. It challenges me to think about how I can do something to please her each week. This forces me to put myself into her shoes. Usually, it is more than just a present that comes out of this. I listen to her better. I am more perceptive. This little exercise is a great blessing for me and for our relationship.

Workshop: Habitual goals

Identify your habits and discover the amazing effects of carefully chosen habitual goals.

1. Which area of your life do you tend to neglect?

_____

_____

_____

2. Where do you regularly cause the most trouble/the greatest damage?

_____

_____

_____

3. What could you do regularly to substitute something more positive for this behavior?

_____

_____

_____

4. Simply pull together a few ideas: What could you do to improve the quality of your life, your work, your relationships? (Please express your ideas as goals.)

_____

_____

_____

Take a critical look at your goals. Are they really goals or are they actually wishes and declarations of intent? How could they be formulated as goals?

Annual good habits training plan

We can give you two more instruments to help you with your long-term development: the Annual training plan and the Masterplan.

Annual training plan

The Annual training plan is a list of habits that you want to add to your repertoire in the near future. I am glad (as you probably will be as well) that I once got into the good habit of regularly brushing my teeth. There is a whole range of early morning habits that make it easier for people to get things done, even when they are only half-awake in the morning.

The culture of a family functions in a similar way. But it has to be consciously developed and molded. Does everyone do their fair share of domestic chores? It is a terrible effort to hand out all the different jobs that come up in a household time after time. Rotate the unpleasant tasks so that everyone makes an appropriate contribution. Or do you prefer draining, argumentative, petulant discussions whenever something has to be done?

A company's communications and human resources culture also needs to be consciously developed. Those concerned should remember that shaping any culture requires time and practice. How do you celebrate birthdays? How do you spend your Sundays? What kind of exercise routine do you have? It might involve going to the gym from 7pm to 8pm every Tuesday. A married couple I know take a fifteen-minute walk round the block every evening before they go to bed, summer and winter. If you want to give up smoking, we recommend replacing it with another ritual. Why not have a break to eat fruit in the garden, crunch on a carrot or savor a few fine Belgian chocolates on a silver platter?

You will find a grid for your "Annual good habits training plan" on page 196. The focus should, above all, be on your habitual goals. Your plan should be no larger than a sheet of A4 paper. Keep it somewhere you look frequently. Copy things you want to do every day, every week, every month and every year into your daily, weekly, monthly and annual checklists. Each time you plan the corresponding period of time, your checklist should be at your side. You can then set deadlines for your goals.

A few ideas and suggestions may help you complete this workshop.

At work, make it a habit…

- to conduct staff appraisal interviews four times a year
- to always check the previous month's figures on the 10th of every month
- to reserve an hour on the last Friday of each month for planning the next month

- to reserve 30 minutes every Friday for planning the next week
- to make planning the day the first thing you do in the office every morning (10 minutes)
- to go round the office after lunch and have a chat with your staff.

Make it a habit to regularly search for significance by

- taking a day and a half off between Christmas and New Year and around your birthday to think over your life, your sense of balance and your work (dream day)
- taking half a day off each month to get some peace and reflect on the past month and your annual targets
- spending at least 30 minutes every Sunday afternoon reading an inspiring book (like Stephen Covey's *The 7 Habits of Highly Effective People* or Anselm Gruen's *Building Self-Esteem*).

Workshop: My good habits training plan

Decide – as quickly as possible – which new good habits you want to anchor in your life.

Choose headings based on a structure that is meaningful for you. In the interests of your all-round health, you should make sure that the areas Self, Job, Significance and Contacts always appear in at least one form or another.

Do not worry about filling out every single part of the form. Concentrate on identifying and acquiring a few key habits.

Area	Habit	Rhythm
E.g. job	Tidy desk	15 min. before leaving office every day

Benefit from the positive power of habit and use it to overcome bad and destructive habits that reduce your quality of life. It's your life, take charge of it!

Your masterplan

You have done plenty of workshops and learned all sorts of things about yourself. Wouldn't it be good to have all this information available at a glance?

We can offer you a tool for this purpose: the Masterplan. It is intended to show all the central points you have identified, which should be revised at least once a year, on one side of a piece of paper. Apart from this, it will help you to define key areas of your life, formulate goals for them and break those goals down into concrete steps. We recommend that you take out your personal copy, which you will find at the back of this book, and work through it step by step in the suggested order. You will come to appreciate its clarity.

Simply fill in what you already know. Some people put off doing this because they do not think their results are good enough, but that is not what is important. You can always improve it later. Note down as much as you can!

Because a written plan has many advantages:
A written plan...

- takes the burden off your memory, keeping your mind free for other things
- has the psychological effect of self-motivation

- teaches discipline and concentration, making you less likely to get distracted
- can be reviewed rapidly on a regular basis, helping you to monitor progress over the long term
- ensures that plans, projects and unfinished business do not get forgotten (but are carried forward to the next day)
- allows you to demonstrate and record what you have done
- forces you to think clearly
- helps you to keep track of what you are doing.

Workshop: My masterplan

Take a look at your Masterplan, which you will find on pages 200–201. How should you set about drawing up your Masterplan? (You may want to photocopy the masterplan and enlarge it to make it easier to complete.)

- Do the easy bit first: Write the year at the top left. **1** If it is already the last quarter of a year, then fill in your annual goals for the coming year.
- Your second step on the journey to a self-determined future was to explore your own potential. You set out to identify your competences, what motivates you, your personal strengths, your values and your wishes.

  You will have made notes about your skills and qualifications on pages 78–79, your Personal strengths on pages 103–105, your Motivating factors on pages 96–97, your Values on pages 110–112 and your Wishes on pages 125–129. Do not shy away from putting in the effort needed to transfer your results onto your Masterplan; you will then have everything available at a glance. **2**
- What are the key points in your vision of life? From your current perspective, what do you want to have achieved by the end of your life? Now write in the life motto you have chosen. **3** For example,

Jörg W. Knoblauch's life motto is "Work hard, pray hard, give people vision." What could your (at least provisional) motto be?

- Next we have left you space for what you have learned from the other workshops. ❹ Maybe you will want to use this part of your Masterplan to write in something from the "Family inheritance" section (pages 66–68), new habits that you want to acquire this year (page 195–196) or ways you want to reward yourself (page 238).

- Now copy your life periods into your Masterplan. ❺ You will remember that you have divided your life into seven-year periods and given each stage a different heading. You will find the headings for the previous periods of your life on page 77, while your future life periods will be noted on page 147.

- What are your personal roles? What are your main tasks? What are the central areas of your life?

  What is meant by personal roles? Are you married? Then you have a role as a husband or wife. Do you have children? Then you have a role as a father or mother. Do you have a job? That is another role. Do you have hobbies? Each hobby you pursue actively is a role. Maybe you have a large fruit garden behind your house that keeps you busy? Maybe you have parents who need caring for? Maybe your finances are causing you headaches because you have to sort out your inheritance arrangements? Maybe you live in a house that needs building work doing to it and demands your attention every weekend? All these require you to play different roles.

  Now decide on the main tasks required by your central life roles and copy them into your Masterplan under ❻. An example will illustrate how this can be done.

- Next comes the important question: What do you want to have achieved in these central areas by the end of your life? ❼

- Think about your next period of your life, maybe the years between 42 and 49. What do you want to have achieved by the end ofthat time? What heading have you given this period? ❽

Masterplan for the year _____ **❶**

My life motto: **❸** _____

My ultimate goal: _____

Results from the   a) **❹** _____   b) _____   c) _____
other Workshops :   _____   _____   _____

My lifeline (7-year periods): What do I want to achieve in each period? **❺**

```
0          7          14         21         28         35
|‖‖‖‖‖‖‖|‖‖‖‖‖‖‖|‖‖‖‖‖‖‖|‖‖‖‖‖‖‖|‖‖‖‖‖‖‖|
```

Personal roles (Main tasks / responsibilities)	What do I want to have achieved by the end of my life? (Ultimate goal)	What do I want to have achie by the end of the current peri Period from _____ to _____
🔔 Role 1: **❻**	1. _____ **❼**	1. _____
🔔 Role 2:	2. _____	2. _____
🔔 Role 3:	3. _____	3. _____
🔔 Role 4:	4. _____	4. _____
🔔 Role 5:	5. _____	5. _____
🔔 Role 6:	6. _____	6. _____
🔔 Role 7:	7. _____	7. _____

❷	Skills and qualifications required Pages 78–79	Motivating factors Pages 96–97	Personal strengths from DISC profile Pages 103–105	Personal values Pages 110–112	Wishes Selected from pages 125–129

```
49          56          63          70          77          84
|  |  |  |  |  |  |  |  |  |  |  |  |  |  |  |  |  |  |  |  |  |  |  |  |
```
❶

This year
Year: _____
Age: _____ Years
❾

1. _____
2. _____
3. _____
4. _____
5. _____
6. _____
7. _____

Next year
Year: _____
Age: _____ Years
❿

1. _____
2. _____
3. _____
4. _____
5. _____
6. _____
7. _____

This year in quarters

	1st quarter	2nd quarter	3rd quarter	4th quarter
1.				
2.				
3.				
4.				
5.				
6.				
7.				

Personal roles (main tasks/life areas)	What do I want to have achieved by the end of my life?	What do I want to have achieved by the end of the current period?
Role 1 Husband	My wife is my best friend	Support Karen as she goes back to work
Role 2 Father	Hand the company on to Ben	Make sure Ben gets the best possible education
Role 3 Manager	Make the company, with its unique philosophy, the number one on the market in its sector	– Cut production costs by 10 percent – Introduce lean organizational structures
Role 4 Member of town council	Resolve the most important conflicts between the younger and older generations in the town	– Set up working party – Build up contacts with the three youth groups
Role 5 Church officer	Help to create an attractive community that attracts people from further away	The church's core activities should convey a shared vision
Role 6 Amateur cook	Write and publish a successful cookbook with recipes from all over the world	Learn about French cuisine in France
Role 7 Health/Fitness	Be able to say, "I have always done the best for my health"	Run for 30 minutes without getting out of breath

- Now to the current or forthcoming year. What has to be done this year to ensure you make progress towards the most important goal you have identified for the next few years? **9**
- What steps will you have to take next year? For example, if you want to have building work done on your house next year, you will have to start taking this into account in your financial planning right now. **10**

- Finally, break down your plan into concrete quarterly steps. ⑪ How much will you have to save in the first quarter to pay for a new conservatory? How much in the second quarter?

Does this strike you as very time-consuming, a lot of trouble, like working on a major project? Use your regular dream day to refine your Masterplan!

Managing priorities through weekly planning

The week is the perfect planning period. A single weekday is far too short to fit in everything important. But you need to find room for it over the course of a week. Anything you do not have time for is not a key area of your life, but at best an optional extra that tends to get overlooked. Of course, there are some exceptions – think of your holidays. However, particularly in the interests of your life balance, you should invest in four main areas (Work, Relationships, Health, Significance) each week. The same is true of the other central areas of your life.

You will gain balance, composure and time for the essential if you define a concrete focus or clear goal for each central area of your life every week. What could you do this week to exploit the Pareto rule and get closer to your annual goal? If you plan your priorities on a weekly basis, you will be able to pull off the balancing act between vision and action. What is decisive in achieving this is that you first practice defining appropriate time windows and deadlines for all the important activities leading to your goal. Many of our contemporaries allow themselves to be governed by a sense of urgency. What is important in their lives is given the little time they have left over. This is a good moment to remember the pebble principle: put the big stones – the real priorities in your life – into the jar first. There will be enough space between them for the pebbles, sand and water!

A weekly plan based on this principle that sets priorities and defines time windows for the genuinely important things in your life is the key to a balanced approach to time management and planning. You can never do everything that would be meaningful, possible and useful. But you must make the best use you can of the time available to you. You will be able to do this if you are aware of your talents and your vocation, keep the end in view from the very beginning, take time for what is truly important and develop a responsible sense of balance. If the important things are not just somewhere at the back of your mind, but actually set down in writing, you will find it easier to say no to demands that are urgent but unimportant. Plan deadlines for yourself and enter them definitively in your time planning system (your personal organizer or kitchen calendar, for example). These deadlines should have just as much weight as many other supposedly important things. Once a deadline has been noted down, it can no longer be so easily pushed aside by daily business. As a result of the vagaries of everyday life, your time will often be occupied with other people's priorities. What is important then gets put to one side in favor of something urgent. Once again: block out the time required for your key areas and tasks well in advance!

You can also plan your week in such a way that you allocate each area of your life to a particular weekday. In any event, you must stay flexible on a day-to-day level. It is a matter of moving in the right direction, not sticking slavishly to a plan. The weekly compass has proved its worth as an aid to putting this approach into practice. Use this form to summarize your weekly priorities for the various areas of your life on a narrow strip of paper that can be stored in a transparent plastic envelope between your conventional daily and weekly plans.

Weekly compass

Date/Week

Life balance

Fitness

Work

Contacts

Significance

Role

Activities

Role

Activities

Role

Activities

Role

Activities

Role

Activities

Your weekly compass

Organizing your day effectively

Of course, it is an enormous help not just to plan each week, but each day as well. This saves time and energy. We will now provide you with a couple of tips for daily planning. How you plan your day will depend a great deal on your situation at work. But remember: planning does not mean imposing a rigid corset that eliminates any trace of flexibility from your schedule; rather it means consciously organizing your life yourself instead of letting others control it for you.

The most important thing first: never drift through your working day (you should not really drift through your day even when you are on holiday). Do not begin your day's work by reading your post or e-mails. Otherwise you will fall into the urgency trap sooner than you would imagine. Begin the day with a brief planning session. What is coming up today? What do I definitely want to achieve? Of course, it may happen that there is something in your post that demands your full attention straightaway. If this is the case, you can take a conscious decision to abandon your original plan for the day and dedicate yourself to a task that has higher priority. You always need this kind of flexibility. However, people who do not begin the day by planning what they want to do are leaving themselves open to having their priorities dictated by others.

Daily planning takes time. Five to ten minutes will be sufficient. But if you invest these minutes systematically, you will save yourself far more time. Because by doing this you are building a protective shield against the people and things that will tend to take up your attention. This will enable you to schedule activities that demand concentration for the right time windows. Consequently, you will work faster, prepare better for appointments and deal with assignments more effectively. A few minutes planning in the morning will be the best investment you can make. Your daily plan is like a map of your day. First thing in the morning, you will develop an idea of where you want to be, when – geographically, but above all intellectually. This alone will influence your thinking and make you work more purposefully.

If you already have experience of weekly planning, you can apply similar principles day by day. The widely used five-step method explained below has proved its worth because it pulls together everything you will need to do.

1. **List your tasks.** Summarize the most important things you have to manage during the day. Some items will already have been scheduled in advance, like the meeting at 11 am or your adult education class in the evening. You are free to decide when you want to work on other matters. You also need to think about the important things you did not have time for yesterday in spite of all your good planning. Allow for calls and letters you will need to respond to today.

2. **Estimate how long things will take.** Calculate roughly the time that will probably be required for each task. Do not be too generous when you do this. It has long been observed that people often need as much time to perform a task as they are allowed for it. So feel free to put yourself under a little pressure.

3. **Reserve buffer times.** As a rule of thumb, plan no more than 60 percent of your working time. Something always happens to

distract your attention from what you are supposed to be doing – surprisingly long telephone conversations, queries from another department, unforeseen changes. It therefore makes no sense to plan more than five hours of an eight-hour day. On the one hand, five hours are horrifyingly little time. On the other, if you manage to concentrate hard on really important things for five hours each working day you will get more done than most of your colleagues in an unplanned ten-hour day.

4. Take decisions. As you always have more to do than is humanly possible, it is better to decide straightaway: What do you want to make your priority today? Which task do you want to cut short? What can be delegated so that you do not have to do it yourself? By this point, you will have realized yet again how important visions and long-term goals are. If you keep them in mind, you will usually find it easier to decide what your highest priority is each day.

5. Write down what you decide in your daily plan and review it later. Check what you have achieved at the end of the working day. If something has not worked out, make sure you have a clear idea of the reasons why. This is the only way to improve your planning. Carry forward items that have not been dealt with to the next day.

Using a modern personal organizer will make it considerably easier to apply this five-step method. If it is intelligently designed, it will provide you with sections where you can put together overviews of your goals, annual, weekly and daily plans, to-do lists and other information. Everything you need to make your life and career plans a reality will be gathered together in one place.

Remember your performance curve when you draw up your daily plan. Most people are not capable of performing at a high level after lunch, so it is best to plan routine tasks (going through the post, reading magazine articles, tidying up) between 1 and 2 pm. Only look at incoming e-mails two or three times a day. Most of them are junk anyway. Today, e-mails are probably more damaging to business than corruption and are a constant source of distraction. Do not allow them to disturb your concentration.

Another tip: If we find a task unpleasant, we tend to put it off – no matter how important it is. You should therefore decide to deal with one of these unpleasant tasks in the morning. This may mean calling up your company's most difficult client or supplying documentation you have to provide for the neighboring depart-ment. You will feel better once you have ticked off this item. You will have cleared another bit of mental clutter out of your mind and will now be able to dedicate yourself to the tasks you actually enjoy with a greater sense of freedom.

Daily planning offers you many advantages. It makes the day manageable and allows you to develop the calm, collected approach you need. You will avoid unnecessary time pressure, while the certainty that you are working on really important tasks will motivate you and make you both more effective and more efficient. If you also plan in activities to maintain your life balance on the different days of the week, you will have taken an important step towards a self-determined future.

The better we organize and plan our day, the better we can use it for the goals we have set ourselves.

The seven fundamental rules for daily planning:

1. Most importantly: write everything down.
   Note all your activities, tasks and deadlines straightaway in your personal organizer. Only then will you be able to keep track of what is going on at all times and concentrate on the essential.
2. Plan your next working day the evening before.
   Make the most of your subconscious and allow its creative powers to work away overnight.
3. Estimate how much time will be needed and set time limits.
   Every financial budget has to be calculated in some way. Remember that time is even more valuable than money! A rough estimate is better than no estimate at all. So:
4. Do not plan the whole day (50/50 rule).
   As a matter of principle, a realistic daily plan should only contain what you want – and are able – to do on the day in question. Less is more! Leave 40 to 50 percent of the day as buffer times. Experience will teach you what you can manage and plan for in your daily working routine – and what is out of the question.
5. Combine activities of the same kind into blocks of work and time and give your day an outline structure – but stay flexible!
   Your daily schedule could look something like this:

> 8.30–10.00 am: Work on an A task (concentrated work without interruptions or calls)
> 10.00–11.00 am: Communication break (discuss queries with staff, telephone calls)
> 11.00–12.00 am: Work on an A task or discussions/meetings (never longer than 1 hour)
> 12.00 am–1.00 pm: Lunch break

1.00–2.00 pm: Social communication, go through post, read trade magazines, C tasks
2.00–3.00 pm: Work on a B task (concentrated work without interruptions or calls)
3.00–4.00 pm: Communication break (discuss queries with staff, telephone calls)
4.00–5.00 pm: B task or discussions/meetings (never longer than 1 hour)
5.00–5.30 pm: Review of the day and daily plan, preparations for next day, leave work

6. Focus systematically on your priorities.
   Ask yourself the following questions again and again. What is really essential? What will take me closer to my goals? What would happen if I passed over this item and did not act on it?
7. Begin, manage and end your day positively.

Your inner attitude will determine your behavior and that of those around you. Think, act and live positively. Enjoy your success.

Learning to relax

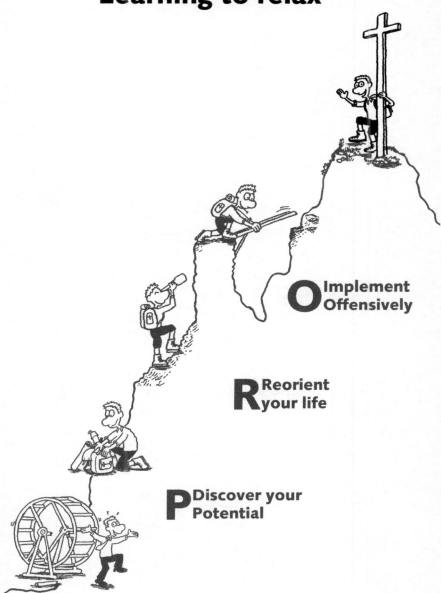

O Implement Offensively

R Reorient your life

P Discover your Potential

Give each day the chance to be
the best day of your life.

Mark Twain

You have reached the summit of the mountain. Now you know how
to realize your dreams and goals in life. If you have taken the exertions
of the last chapter upon yourself, you will be like a potter who has
labored to get his heavy potter's wheel moving. He has to pedal hardest
at the beginning. Later it is enough for him to nudge the pedal gently
with his foot – and the wheel keeps spinning round. To stay with this
image, your life is being molded on the potter's wheel. You have
resolved to improve your life, refine it and make it more beautiful. The
foundations for this have been laid in the previous chapters.

Maybe you asked yourself in the middle of the process: Is it
worth all this effort to think so intensively about all these deep,
meaningful questions? Much more probably, however, with every
chapter and every workshop you will have become increasingly
aware of the dynamic you generate when you set out into a self-
determined future. If you have made it as far as this page, if you
have really done the work asked of you, then you will have left the
hamster's wheel far behind and experienced a new feeling of
liberation. You will have broken out from the treadmill of a model
imposed on you by others and set out to live a life of balance. Now
you must do everything to ensure that nothing pushes your life and
career planning back in the other direction. The hamster's wheel is
not a good place – either for you or for anyone else.

You have now answered the central question concerning your goal in life for the time being. But you can only ever start from what you know today. As this knowledge changes, you may also alter your long-term goals with the passing of time. This will only be proof of your continuing development and personal maturity. This is why the process that you have gone through with us is not so much a one-off undertaking as a model of how to carry out regular reviews of your goals and approach to life. You will benefit most from it if you take this book off the shelf at least twice a year, add to your notes and apply the PRO formula to yourself repeatedly in order to shape your life responsibly and proactively.

Now it is important to keep the potter's wheel spinning. If you have carelessly let it grind to a halt, it will be much more difficult to build up the momentum again. You probably understand better now why we recommended that you enter your dream days in your diary at regular intervals. Dream days are particularly necessary if you want to live a balanced life. And you will find them more and more enriching each time you take one. On your first dream day, you will work on the basic questions of your life and start to clarify them. You can then get down to the detailed work on the dream days that follow. Your life will become more fulfilled, more significant and more intense. If you reflect on the various roles you play in life on your dream day, you will always get yourself back on track again. You will travel in the right direction and drift off course less and less from quarter to quarter. This certainty is an important source of calm. By contrast, meaningless activity for its own sake is a cause of ill health.

Becoming an artist of life

How will you become an artist of life? You will gather your first experiences as an apprentice and qualify as a journeyman by coping with the challenges thrown up by normal, everyday life. Even Michelangelo was once an apprentice. His master came to him one day and smashed a wonderful statue he had just created with the words, "Mark you, talent is cheap, dedication is gold." By doing this he showed, in an admittedly rough and ready fashion, that it is not sufficient to give your creativity free rein. You have to put in hard work to transcend merely good results and achieve something truly outstanding. Even if you do not favor educational methods of this kind, the principle is correct. A person of average gifts will be far superior to an inconsistent genius when it comes to implementing plans systematically. Become an artist, let your life be an artwork, work hard on it! That will ensure you a fulfilled life – it *is* a fulfilled life.

Being an artist in daily life is not an easy matter. There will inevitably be unpleasant surprises and disasters from time to time. We only have to think of the terrible flooding that struck East Germany, Austria and the Czech Republic in 2002. The dreams, values and visions of many hard-working people were quite literally swept away by these floods.

We came to know one 57-year-old artist of life at a seminar we ran. It was impressive how responsibly he dealt with his life, his wife and his grown-up children. He had been a chemist working for the same company for many years. One morning, his 35-year-old colleague stood in the office fighting back tears. When asked why he was so downcast, the younger man said, "I have just been made redundant. In six weeks, I will have to leave the company. They no longer have enough work for everyone. I have a mother who needs caring for, my wife is pregnant with our third child, we're building our own house…" After listening sympathetically to his distressed colleague, our artist of life took his leave. Following a long telephone conversation with his wife, he disappeared. A little later, the head of the company came to the 35-year-old and said, "Your redundancy notice is being withdrawn. Your colleague has offered to go in your place. He has already paid off his mortgage and can always take early retirement if he doesn't find any suitable work." This artist of life told us his story during a "life curve workshop." It was clear to him that he would not find a job that would match his aspirations. But he came to our seminar to reflect on how he could develop his life further in a responsible way. He had earned the money for the seminar doing temporary work, but he and his wife were still certain they had done the right thing.

It is not always easy to do the right thing. It does not have to be as heroic as this man's story. But it costs effort to manage everyday life consistently and responsibly. However, we promise you that once you have "tasted" this approach you will not want any other wine to pass your lips. It is a great danger to compare yourself with others. Envy is the number one destroyer of happiness. Always looking at other people and tormenting yourself with the mad idea that everyone else is doing better than you are will wear you down in the end. What is important is living authentically and, on this basis, shaping your own life with a sense of personal responsibility, even if your neighbor does have a slightly larger car.

You have identified what is important for you, then related it to the concrete task of daily planning. But this should not mean you just swap one hamster's wheel for another. You are not competing for glory in a race to achieve a more efficient lifestyle. What is really at stake is a self-determined future and a balanced life in which even unforeseen events will at most distract you from your true goal. Learn to enjoy taking a relaxed approach.

However, being an artist of life also means taking new risks and not just assessing every step you take by whether it fits in with your idea of safety. "There are no certainties in life, just opportunities" said Mark Twain. We have observed again and again that some people "change down" a gear in the second half of their lives. They switch to another job, some even move to a different country. Superficially, this damages their chances of success. But when they take these decisions, they give their lives new direction and enrich them in ways that cannot be measured in material terms.

The American poet Robert Frost wrote, "Two roads diverged in a wood, and I – / I took the one less traveled by, / And that has

made all the difference." Only a true artist of life could have composed these lines! Anyone who always follows the well-traveled road may well pass his or her days in relative security. But this risk-averse thinking will prevent them from seeing new opportunities. You have got to take a few risks if you really want to get the best out of life. This is not intended as a plea for unreasonable behavior. Rather, we are suggesting that people should cast off the shackles that stop them from becoming real artists of life. We agree with Norman Vincent Peale, an old master of optimism: "Throw your heart over the fence and the rest will follow."

Nobody enjoys someone who cannot enjoy

You have broken out of the hamster's wheel. Now when you exert yourself, you are no longer turning a wheel round and round, but moving forward step by step with firm ground under your feet. However, this will not satisfy you in the long term if you do not give yourself appropriate opportunities to recover from your efforts – times of peace and relaxation.

The Bible begins with the familiar story of the Creation, which actually has quite a surprising ending. First, it describes how God created the world in six days. Incidentally, the word that stands for "day" in the original text can also mean any "period of time." The Creation was not complete at the end of the first day. It was allowed to develop. And what happened on the seventh day? Did God, who is said to have created people in his own image, order them to take a day of rest? Certainly not! According to the first book of the Bible, God Himself rested on the seventh day.

An important experience runs through the whole of human history: We humans do not exist solely to work. Even when we are resting, we reflect on something divine. Creativity is important, it is part of the essence of humanity. Our health suffers if we cannot express our creative impulses. As consultants, we have advised many people who did not really need to work any more from a financial point of view. However, after enjoying parties and month-long holidays for a while, they would feel a growing desire to be creative, to contribute with their labor to making the world a little better.

We humans need a balance between work and rest. Lack of rest kills creativity and causes health problems. Working six days a week is quite enough: enjoy the seventh! During the French Revolution, the Revolutionaries tried to introduce a ten-day week by decree, but it was never accepted. Imagine you only had one day off in ten! Creativity depends on rest, although most people find it difficult to ever get any peace and quiet. But there is a surprising dynamic that comes from simply sitting for a while, reading a good book, enjoying a film, having time for yourself, watching the clouds...

Once again: the weekly day of rest is a very important part of a relaxed way of life. Please do not get stressed out on Sundays. It is better to write a script for "your" Sunday, deciding exactly what you want to do and when. If you regularly have to work on Sundays, then choose another day of rest, but do take one day off a week, for your own good and for the good of those around you! If you are well rested, even unpleasant surprises will cause much less disruption to your plans. If you are tense, you are far more likely to overreact to disappointments. We all tend to keep the lid on our feelings during the week – if the pressure builds up too much, they can explode in your face.

Families are popular today, even though or possibly because relationships break down more frequently than ever before. But families cost energy and small children can be very demanding. Do not allow yourself to be a victim of this energy-sapping situation. Make sure you have opportunities to relax. If you are bringing up children on your own, you could have them looked after by a babysitter one half-day a week so you can enjoy some sleep, read a good book in peace or drink coffee with a friend. It is easier for married couples. Give each other some time off every week so you can sleep properly or simply enjoy time to yourself.

There is another reason why we need rest periods. We need to protect our minds against overstimulation. You will be surprised how good it feels to reserve one day of the week for peace, contemplation, thought and relaxation. This is especially important if you find it very difficult to switch off. Nobody enjoys being with someone who cannot enjoy life! Do not put your pleasures on hold.

Take time to enjoy the perfume of the roses

Take time to think, it is the source of power.
Take time for work, because this is the price of success.
Take time to play, this is the secret of youth.
Take time to read, this is the foundation of knowledge.
Take time for devotion, it washes the earthly dust from your eyes.
Take time to dream, this is the path to the stars.
Take time to laugh, this helps us bear life's burdens.
Take time for love, it is the true wealth of life.
Take time to look around you, the day is too short to be selfish.
Take time to meet your friends and help them, this is the source of happiness.
Time is the most limited resource you have.
So take time to enjoy the perfume of the roses.

Irish

We know a number of women and men who take half an hour every day not just for relaxation, but to enjoy the little things in life. They are all extremely nice and could certainly not be described as malingerers. They make the most of their talents and have brilliantly mastered the balance between work and rest. One good friend sat in a café for an hour after parking his new car on the opposite side of the street. He ordered a cappuccino and enjoyed gazing at his new acquisition. Do you find this too materialistic? Others love going into their children's rooms at night and looking at them while they sleep. There is so much beauty in the world – dancing snowflakes, glorious meadows full of wildflowers, your own husband or wife…

Nature offers us endless opportunities to replenish our reserves. When was the last time you picked a green leaf from a tree? When was the last time you went out to watch a sunrise or sunset near your home? When did you last walk barefoot through a meadow? The refreshing moments that creation grants us are enormously undervalued. Walking on a windy day, identifying the songs of different birds, playing in the snow – all this makes life richer. And it doesn't cost a cent.

Celebrating life

There is another clever idea that helps us enjoy life: celebrating. It is easy to find reasons to celebrate: an exam passed, the baptism of your youngest child, a salary rise or the sale of a car at a profit.

People have always sensed the importance of celebrating. The beginning of spring, for example, when the days started to get longer again, and the gathering of the harvest in autumn were traditionally occasions to give thanks and celebrate. Some of these traditions have been lost now that many of us have our harvest

transferred automatically to our bank accounts. Year in, year out, we live without any true appreciation of the many valuable gifts everyday life brings us. One family we know should be an example to us all. Every Saturday evening, they celebrate another working week completed. The parents and children sit down together, the table is set festively and they eat a special meal, then there are sweets and a games evening or a good film. For this family, Saturday evening has become the pivotal point of the whole week.

Defeats also need to be celebrated. Bury them ceremoniously. If you do not deliberately mourn for losses, there is a danger that your feelings of sadness will be released in an uncontrolled fashion. It is better to make a conscious decision to enjoy a luxurious dessert as a wake for a piece of bad luck than plunder the fridge out of frustration. If your company has had to report unexpected losses, you could sit at your desk for weeks with a miserable face. Or you could organize a bring-a-dish party with your staff that takes some of the sting out of this negative experience and encourages them to take new initiatives and do their best again. Your losses can be "buried" symbolically at your party, for example, by burning a piece of paper with the most horrible figures written on it. Maybe

this will strike you as a little crazy. But the alternative is to wallow in your suffering for ages without this necessarily improving the situation in the least. So celebrate your defeats.

Happy Birthday! There are very few people who do not feel something special on this day. You are a unique individual, an original. Your very existence is reason to celebrate. Maybe difficult living circumstances sometimes obscure this truth. But despite that, life is a gift! Celebrate it! Do not let social constraints of any kind pressurize you into celebrating your birthday in a particular way. It is your day. If you do not want to cater for your guests at home, enjoy an evening with your best friends at a nice restaurant.

Do you have a calendar of your personal celebrations? On which day did you get to know your wife? Take a day off work for your wedding anniversary and do something fun together! You can also celebrate the anniversary of the day your company was founded with your staff. The pressure of work makes it easy to forget our gratitude for the positive things that employment brings with it: a job, a living wage every month, pleasant colleagues and satisfied clients. My car dealer makes the most of it whenever he has to hand over a new company car to me. He treats it as a little party, congratulates us on our new car, presents us with a bottle of champagne and a little gift (usually a model of the new car) and celebrates the occasion. I am coming to enjoy this more and more. Of course, I am pleased with my new car – so why not celebrate it as well?

The last school day before the summer holidays is always a time of celebration in our family. Regardless of how the exam results have turned out, we celebrate the passing of another school year with all its victories and defeats.

In addition to the birthdays of his staff, one manager I know has recorded all the dates they joined the company in his calendar. Every time one of these dates comes around, he visits the person in question at their workplace with a little present, tells them what he appreciates about them and thanks them for their contribution. Some of his colleagues commented on his little ritual by saying, "He doesn't really need to do all this, but we wouldn't like him to stop either."

Draw up your own calendar of celebrations you enjoy every year – which could include a romantic weekend, attending a ball or visiting a street festival. There are also special occasions I celebrate all on my own and no one else knows about! Celebrating is an expression of appreciation. Appreciation is connected with gratitude and awakens our consciousness of how rich our life actually is: in people, in the wonders of nature, in history. Gratitude liberates us to enjoy the moment. We can become obsessed with always reaching out for what is ahead of us and not even notice the present any more. Guard yourself against this dangerous virus.

Preparing an event (with others) is just as important as the celebration itself. Sometimes it is terrible how preparations for celebration can be overshadowed by the stress they induce. This is not what we mean! Find the style of celebration that is right for you. Then you will regain a sense of the richness of life.

The five languages of love

The biggest differences are often revealed when people are preparing a joint celebration. We humans are simply very diverse. Some want to get married in a small chapel high up in the mountains surrounded by only their closest friends and family. Others are disappointed that the banqueting suite of the local country house hotel has room for only 350 wedding guests.

A good friend of ours, Gary Chapman, is a marriage guidance counselor by profession. He used to take notes on all his discussions with couples and would browse through them again afterwards. When he did this, he made an interesting discovery. He noticed that it was unusually common for one of the spouses to say that he would tear out both his eyes for the other, that he made every conceivable effort to show his partner that he loved her, but that nothing he did seemed to make any impact on her.

Chapman thought about how such misunderstandings can arise and came up with a revealing explanation. There are different languages of love! Consequently, it can appear as if one partner is speaking to the other in Chinese even though she understands only English. He talks until he is blue in the face, but she cannot understand a thing he says. She tries to demonstrate her love to him, but he does not even notice she is trying to tell him something.

A woman whose relationship with her father was very important to her complained she always yearned for some sign of love from him, but he never showed anything, not even the tiniest hint of affection. "My father is completely indifferent to me" was her painful conclusion. By chance, I had a conversation with the father a few weeks later. He was frustrated because his daughter gave him the feeling that he meant nothing to her at all. Evidently, the two were completely failing to communicate with each other.

In one company, a manager gave up his efforts to get on with one of his staff. He felt that he appreciated his colleague and tried to convey this to him. The employee had also given up on the relationship. Despite working extremely hard, he could not see any appreciation expressed in his manager's behavior. Each revealed his distress in one-to-one discussions. You should not believe that mutual appreciation is unimportant to employees in business. Of course, it plays a different role in a partnership, but cooperation and relationships of trust in the workplace are impossible without it.

Chapman spent a great deal of time studying this phenomenon and the misunderstandings that were obviously taking place. He wrote up his ideas in a book that was, in fact, intended primarily as an aid for his clients. You can imagine his amazement when, without a great deal of effort on his part, 1.5 million copies were sold worldwide and he started receiving letters from all corners of the globe telling him how much his publication had helped a range of people. His insight was that each of us has a love language that we use to communicate our affection in a quite individual way. Chapman describes five languages.

Language 1: Acts of service. Do you know people who express their sympathy with others through their willingness to serve? They iron clothes, bake, cook and clean in order to make someone else's life nicer. Sometimes, all this bustle just annoys the other person, and the affection it expresses appears not to be understood. "What else can I do to show you that I love you?" wonders a man who wishes to serve his partner. "If you really loved me, you would tell me, you would express it in words," could be his wife's answer, "The last time you told me you loved me was 20 years ago – which shows how indifferent you have become towards me." Can you sense the misunderstandings and the massive potential for conflict inherent in this situation?

Some people speak the language of Acts of service and are always thinking about how they can do even more to demonstrate what their partner means to them. The same thing also happens in organizations and friendships. Many work not just to get something done, but also to express their appreciation for somebody. Appreciation is the oil that keeps the gears of our souls running smoothly.

Language 2: Words of affirmation. The love language spoken by the woman in the example above is Words of affirmation. She yearns for spoken words, for a handwritten card, for her partner to tell her how much he appreciates her. You can probably think of people who mainly express their affection through words: "That's a pretty dress you're wearing today," "I like how courteously you deal with our clients," "I love you, son." These are the ways a person whose preferred love language is Words of affirmation will show their sympathy with others.

At the beginning of this section, we discussed the tense relationship between a manager and one of his employees. The drama played out between the two was rooted in the fact that the

employee primarily expressed his sympathy through Acts of service, while the manager felt his attempts to serve were rather over the top. In return, the employee expected the same from his superior. The compliments the manager gave him were not understood. "Words, nothing but empty words," his assistant believed.

However, there are positive examples as well. One year, a large company put very different levels of investment into its various departments. One department received almost nothing. However, the management consistently used Words of affirmation in this part of the organization. A year later, there was great amazement throughout the company when it became apparent that there had been a staggering increase in this department's productivity. The climate of recognition and mutual praise had transformed the employees there into a highly motivated team.

Language 3: Exclusive quality time. For some people, words are just empty talk. They believe that, "If someone likes me, they will take time for me." Exclusive quality time is another love language some of us speak. These people give others time and attention and like to do things as a couple. They love sharing experiences and spending time with each other. In one company, it was regarded as the highest sign of approval from the management to be allowed to go along on a business trip. The shared journey and visit to the client were certainly not wonderful experiences in themselves, but the love language of the employees involved made them very positive occasions.

Language 4: Physical touch. Have you ever noticed that there are some people who place great emphasis on greeting others with a handshake? Someone called my name not long ago when I was in town! He ran up to me, grasped my hand, then shook it and shook it and shook it. I wanted to pull my hand away, but the other person gripped it tightly, beaming with pleasure and telling me how nice it was to meet me there. It was only with great difficulty that I succeeded after a while in extricating my hand from his grasp.

There are people who, without the slightest impropriety, love touching others, shaking hands, patting friends on the back and putting an arm round someone's shoulders. Physical touch is a very important love language for many of us.

You can observe this even at a supermarket. There are shop assistants who slam your change uncaringly onto the counter, while others let it drop a couple of feet into your hand from above, and there are some who are happy to brush your palm as they count out your coins. The Germans, for example, are comparatively reserved about touching others, quite unlike their Italian neighbors to the south. In Italy, people are far less inhibited about physical contact and it is much more a part of everyday life. One study found that at business meetings between Germans the participants touch each other twice on average: shaking hands when they meet and when they say goodbye. Even this does not happen every time. In comparable situations in Italy, those present touch each other at least ten times during each meeting.

We are aware that this issue is a constant cause of anxiety in many parts of the world. However, the language described here has nothing to do with sexuality. What is important is the symbolic and communicative power of touch, while what is appropriate can vary very widely depending on the type of relationship. Indeed, the same is true of all love languages!

Language 5: Gifts. The fifth love language is that of Gifts. I myself understand this love language particularly well. I take special pleasure in giving other people gifts. If I am on my way to a client, I am always subconsciously looking for a little present – a book that could help him further, jelly beans for his children... It is just as important to me to keep giving little gifts to my wife. Not a week goes by without me surprising her with some little token of my appreciation. This is my way of showing affection, interest and sympathy. And of course, I understand this language very well when my partner uses it to tell me how she feels.

Chapman compares this emotional dynamic with a love tank. Imagine we all have a tank in our heart where we store love and affection. The fuller it is, the more we feel loved, the more fulfilled we feel our relationships to be. To clarify: each person needs to fill their love tank with all five love languages, but different people may need widely varying amounts of the same language. Maybe there are one, two or three languages that are particularly important for you, while others play lesser roles. However, your tank may always be well filled with one language that is significant to you. It will then be all the more important to include the others in your life.

Workshop: Five languages of love

Which is the most important language for you? Which is the least important? Please rank them in order of preference.

Love language	What expression of affection do I most appreciate from my partner?	How do I like to express my own affection?	Example	
			Me	My wife
Acts of service			2	3
Words of affirmation			3	2
Quality time			5	1
Physical touch			4	5
Gifts			1	4

As examples, this table lists my love languages (left) and those of my wife (right, the numbers indicate their order of importance for us). You may find it surprising, but we prefer quite different languages. This is no reason for concern as long as both partners are aware of these differences.

My eldest son expresses his affection primarily through physical touch. He likes to sit on my lap or wrap my arm round his shoulders. By contrast, his father likes to express his affection with gifts. Our daughter said once in the heat of the moment, "Keep your stupid presents, no one wants them anyway." I was insulted, she was disappointed. She was yearning for a couple of nice words or a compliment. Just once, she said, she wanted to hear, "Daughter of mine, I love you." For her father, words were not so important because he felt he expressed his affection more than enough through his gifts, which were very generous. It is sometimes shocking how people can completely fail to understand each other.

Which is your preferred love language? You must make sure you use it because it is very important for you. Give your partner gifts in your language and theirs as well! I show my wife my love with little presents because this is my language; and I give her quality time, which is her language, because doing things as a couple is extremely important for her. Before I was aware of this dynamic, I wasted a great deal of money, time and energy because I wanted to show her my affection in a way she neither wanted nor appreciated. Today, we show each other how we feel in our different languages and have noticed the surprising effect this has: it works!

Reward yourself

There is one person you must certainly not forget when it comes to showing affection in the right love language: yourself! Reward yourself in the language you speak best. There may be many accents and dialects, but you should stick with your language, both in your relations with others and when it comes to your own needs. Fill up your love tank by doing something you enjoy. It will help you to be more relaxed about life, as we will see in this section.

Love your neighbor as yourself. You will certainly be familiar with this fundamental precept from the Bible. These words rightly remind us to consider our neighbors and our environment, and act in ways that benefit them. Brotherly love is not explicitly at the heart of this book, yet we have made it clear several times that your life should never be purely selfish if it is to unfold its positive potential. Thinking of others – my country, my society, my partner, my city and not just myself – is a basic precondition for the healthy functioning of society and the individual. However, only thinking of others and never giving yourself the attention you need will be similarly counterproductive.

The approach we take in this book – helping you to change yourself from someone who is driven by events into someone who makes things happen, to develop from an apprentice into an artist of life – is not an easy one. Hopefully no one promised you it would be a piece of cake! However, it will lead you to a fulfilled life in which you can look at yourself in the mirror every night and say, "I could not have lived this day any better."

How can you love yourself? Working through this book is a healthy form of self-love. As you do the various workshops, you will be endeavoring to take charge of your life, discover and develop your potential and learn how to maintain a healthy balance between the important areas of your life.

Do you reward yourself? I will put the question even more provocatively: how do you reward yourself? When did you last give yourself a treat? As we have said, working on yourself is tough. Of course, every goal you achieve is reward enough in itself. Some experts rightly criticize an excessive concentration on rewards because it runs the risk of relativizing the original goal. However, we have observed that people who regularly reward themselves in a suitable way are much less in danger of succumbing to addiction. Rewarding oneself is part of a "celebratory culture." It is essential if we are to enjoy life. I have friends who give themselves a little present every month. They approach life deliberately and reflectively. At the end of the month they think over their Masterplan, review what they have achieved and carry forward things that have not been dealt with. Then they set about treating themselves. One friend is a passionate music-lover. If he has managed his monthly quota of work, he purchases a new CD for his collection and has it gift-wrapped. After this, his ritual takes him to a nice café on the market place, where he orders a cappuccino and enjoys unwrapping his present in peace. He gives himself a present! A quirk? Maybe. But a healthy quirk that strengthens him in his relaxed approach to life.

What can you do to treat yourself? Some people give themselves a visit to the sauna once a week. Others prefer to eat a gourmet meal. One colleague adds another piece to her expensive coffee service every month – it is now almost complete. There are as many different ways of treating and rewarding yourself as there are people: a good concert, a bottle of fine wine, a model car for your collection, a visit to the cinema, a new plant for your conservatory or an hour playing piano on your own followed by a big slice of gateau to enjoy while you listen to a Mozart piano sonata.

What presents could you give yourself? In the following workshop, we invite you to gather ideas about how you could reward yourself. Of course, you might fancy a round-the-world trip. Here, however, we are much more interested in small, pleasant things you can do *regularly* to treat yourself. On a small scale, this should have a place in your life every day.

Workshop: Self-reward list

Write down what you could do to treat yourself every month (for example, visiting the sauna, eating out)

_____

_____

_____

_____

_____

_____

_____

_____

Encouragement on the way

Imagine you want to reduce your weight by a pound a month because your body is telling you that your built-in hot-water bottle is bad for your health. When are you more likely to be motivated and feel greater pressure to succeed?

- If you decide to do this quietly and secretly in your own room?
- Or if you ask a friend to stand beside you on the first day of every month while you weigh yourself to check your progress?

It may have been seen as a sign of weakness to seek help when coping with various processes of change 20 years ago, but today this is very common, even among top managers. People no longer ask "whether" someone is being helped, but "who" is doing the helping. This development is to be welcomed because it enables people to make better progress. We all have our weaknesses, but most of them are much easier to manage if we provide each other with mutual encouragement and support. Mentoring and coaching are the keywords in this field.

The most common kind of support is probably what is known as co-mentoring. We have been encouraging the participants in our seminars to make use of such learning partnerships for years. A wife and husband may co-mentor each other in the private sphere, colleagues who want to help each other in particular fields may do it at the workplace. We have been delighted to work with companies that changed from places where no one was happy into places where everyone learned from and with each other. Employees recognized the need for change and asked colleagues to encourage them and check on how they were doing during this process. In any such partnership, responsibility lies and remains with the person who wants to change! Any form of relationship based on partnership is outstandingly suitable for co-mentoring.

Of course, you can also employ a professional to support you through important processes. Experience shows that if you do this you will be giving yourself one of the most important keys to sustainable change in your behavior and style of working. In the world of sport, it is completely normal for every sportsman and sportswoman to have a coach who works on their weaknesses with them. In the US, professional coaching is now standard for managers as well. As a rule, the best have not just one, but even two coaches. At an international level, outstanding results have been achieved with this approach to identifying and implementing ideas and ideals.

There is a simple explanation for this success. Anyone who strives for goals without telling others about them will not be subject to effective control. Left to themselves, they will find a thousand reasons why they have fallen short of their goals. And others may not even notice because they had no idea that these goals were being pursued in the first place. Things look different if you regularly talk to a neutral coach. He will ask about the motives behind your goals. He will check your plans to see whether they are achievable. He will want to know exactly why you have not achieved something. A coach performs a kind of strategic control. He does not relieve the coachee of the need to take decisions, but he will test out his or her thinking and actions. Your discussions with a coach will sharpen your perceptions, expand your horizons and motivate you to reach new heights of achievement. Merely knowing that you have a meeting with your coach in two weeks can inspire you to overcome your tendency to procrastinate and encourage you to set about important tasks. A growing number of managers are exploiting this dynamic.

To begin with, it is worth limiting how long you work with a coach (six to ten meetings, on average). These sessions should focus on the resolution of a particular problem, such as "How can I get promotion?" or "How do I create an atmosphere in my department that stimulates my staff to perform at the top level?" There are two different types of coach: the expert who will advise you about a specific problem and the "sparring partner" who will challenge your thinking and actions more generally with questions, criticism and unorthodox suggestions. You should start the coaching process by clarifying what type of coach you need for your problem and which goals you want to achieve. You will work together with the coach to draw up proposals for action that take you closer to solving your problem. Once you have begun implementing these ideas, you will discuss your successes and failures, evaluate your initial results and draw conclusions from them for the way forward.

At the end of this first, limited, period of coaching, you should take stock and define the steps you want to take after you stop seeing your coach. A while later (six months to a year), it may make sense to start a new coaching program.

Of course, you can also cooperate with a coach on an ongoing basis, and you should eventually seek to do this. The risk newcomers to coaching run is that they may rely too much on their coach and, in particular, make the coach responsible for their own failures – even when he could not have done anything about them. A time limit will therefore be helpful while you are being coached because it will heighten your awareness that you will have to manage on your own in the end. Coaching has proved an ideal way of helping people with a wide spectrum of problems, including conflicts within companies as well as the development and implementation of strategies for firms and private individuals. Career planning, a change of job or your complete inability to organize yourself at the office – an external observer, auditor, advisor and sparring partner can give the decisive assistance in these fields that will enable you to make a quantum leap forward. Try it out! You can only benefit.

Incidentally, what are known as "historic mentors" are sometimes overlooked in this connection. These are figures who may already be dead, but whose biographies and life stories encourage us to address similar challenges in our own lives. Some people mention Mahatma Gandhi as a historic mentor, others George Fox, the founder of the Quakers, or the statesman and Enlightenment thinker Benjamin Franklin. Look for your own models. Ask yourself from time to time: How would my historic mentor have reacted if he or she were in my shoes?

Maybe you will find that there are people still alive today who may not be available as personal coaches, but whose thinking and deeds strike you as exemplary and worthy of emulation. Let yourself be inspired by other artists of life.

Your contract with yourself

Although this book is full of positive messages and big promises, the way to a self-determined future is anything but a cozy stroll. The world is full of pressures that will hold you back from reaching your true goal. This will probably have already begun as you worked through the workshops in this book. Tiredness, the claims of your partner and children and the desire for things that take your mind off your problems will have prevented you from completing some of the workshops. But even if you are one of the steadfast who have withstood every distraction, you will know there are many more stones lying in the way that can make you stumble, force you to take a diversion or bring you to a juddering halt. None of this will take you any closer to your goal of a self-determined future.

Anyone who sets out to do something always has three groups of people against him:
those who are against it,
those who don't want to do anything and
those who wanted to do the same thing themselves.

Notice at the Café des Platanes, Ile Rousse, Corsica

"What successful people have in common is the ability to keep the gap between a decision and its implementation extremely narrow," says the psychologist Jürgen Schneider. As an example, he mentions a young man who had fallen in love with a concert pianist. Everything militated against this relationship because the lady of his dreams was not interested in him. All she could think of were her concert tours, and she consequently did not want to get involved in a relationship – let alone marriage. But the young man followed her on her travels and courted her when she performed in Canada and Switzerland. His persistence had its reward: the two are now happily married.

Most men would have given up early on and would probably have backed off after the first rebuff. As a result, however, they would not have enjoyed the fruits of success. The art is to display the maximum of persistence without slipping into grim determination. Persistence implies: I will pursue my goal energetically regardless of what stands in my way. Grim determination implies: I will only be happy once I have reached my goal. Do not make your happiness solely dependent on such successes. Enjoy the process. Sense how the resistance you encounter makes you stronger and how you suddenly find yourself taking new paths that would have remained hidden to you had it not been for these difficulties.

Examples of such persistence being rewarded are legion. It is reported of Walt Disney that he and his ideas were rejected by more than 300 banks. Only the 303rd bank gave him the loan he needed to create Disneyland. Can you imagine how he must have felt at the 301st and 302nd banks? How many associates must have secretly whispered, "Look, there goes Walt Disney, the madman who cannot admit he is pursuing a crazy idea even after being turned down 300 times"? But he did not give up – and finally became a massive success. This is reminiscent of the story of Thomas Edison. While he was developing the light bulb, he carried out about 1,000 failed experiments before he found the filament that met all technical requirements. He did not regard these failed experiments as defeats, but as stations on the way to success. After all, he had discovered 1,000 ways a light bulb *does not* function. That was Edison's creative response to the setbacks he suffered!

We have followed one goal throughout this book. We want to enable you to find a way of determining your own future. The PRO formula has shown you three practical steps towards this end. Now it is up to you. Will you close the book with a gentle smile and carry on as before? Or will you set off on a journey through life following a route that you alone will map out? Will you let yourself be blown off course by the first unfavorable wind? Or will you find your lighthouse? Will you defy adversity and march on unwaveringly to your ultimate goal?

Workshop: Success is a journey – tips on the way

In this last workshop, we will now ask you to decide how you will continue the PRO process. Decide when your next dream days will be, who could act as your mentor or coach, where you will work on your competences and what you want to do to help others.

My next dream days (dates):

_____

Friends who will support me:

- _____
- _____
- _____
- _____
- _____

Who could be my mentor?

- _____
- _____
- _____
- _____
- _____

Who would I like to support?

- _____
- _____
- _____
- _____
- _____

Will this last workshop guarantee you success? Certainly not. Something is still needed that we have deliberately left to the end of the book (page 247): your irrevocable decision to work for a self-determined future, a clear, manageable, measurable decision set down in writing. We have drawn up a declaration for you in which you will undertake to put into practice what you have learned from this book. All you have to do is write in your name, the date, the dates of your next two dream days and the day of the week when you intend to do your weekly planning. And of course you will have to do the most important thing: sign it. We show great respect for the signature in our culture. Tax returns are confirmed, marriages concluded and million-dollar contracts sealed with a signature. It is comparatively difficult to revoke a document once it has been signed. And that is how you should view the following undertaking. You are concluding a contract with yourself. Better still, you are concluding a contract with your own future.

We would encourage you to complete and sign this declaration. Doing this will help you not to leave your life as it has been, but set out for new shores. If you like, you can even make signing it a bit of a celebration. Drink some champagne and sketch out the future you want to attain. Find a witness to whom you can explain the significance of this commitment and who will subsequently remind you of what you have signed. Particularly at times when you seem to be slipping back into the old rut or have obstacles to overcome, recalling this undertaking will help you to give your life direction again. Why on earth should you give up responsibility for the most valuable asset you possess – your life? So decide your future yourself – and sign up!

My commitment

As of today, _____ (date), I, _____
(name), will decide my future myself. I have resolved to
proactively implement what I have learned from this book. I
will consistently reject "life in the hamster's wheel" and work
to gain a clear view of my lighthouse.

In future, I will reserve at least half a day twice yearly for a
dream day on which I will reappraise my potential, my values,
my goals, my habits and my successes. My next two dream days
will be on _____ (date) and _____ (date).
I will also revise the Masterplan for my life on these days.

I have recognized that a self-determined life requires clear
goals and systematic time planning. I have therefore defined
measurable, manageable, motivating goals for each area of my
life, set them down in writing and copied them into my
Masterplan. I will use weekly planning to ensure I lead a
balanced life. In future, I will plan the seven days ahead of me
every _____ (day of week) and take account of all
the important areas of my life when doing so. Furthermore, I
undertake to invest at least five minutes at the beginning of
each working day in daily planning.

I will develop my abilities purposefully and make effective
use of literature, audiobooks, time planning systems and
seminars. I will examine the extent to which a personal coach
could help me on my journey towards a self-determined future.

Above all, I will do something _every day_ that takes me
closer to my goals. I will not let myself be controlled by
others, but persist in giving my life direction _every day_.

_____
				Signature

Afterword

Welcome to the club. You have given your life a new direction and used the PRO formula to successfully start your journey into a self-determined future – it is a high ambition, but manageable. We are delighted that we have been able to accompany you for a while along the way.

We admit that we are curious about your experiences on this journey: about how you describe your "before" and "after." We are so curious that we would like to encourage you to write down your story and send it to us (e-mail: knoblauch@tempus.de). How did you win back control over your own time? What was your first dream day like? And your tenth? The three steps we have taken you through in this book are based on generally valid principles. And yet they will have different effects on the life of each individual.

We hope you succeed in enriching your life, finding fulfillment and learning to relax because you know you have done your best. The future now belongs to you.

Acknowledgments

There are numerous people without whom this book would never have been written. We feel it is important to mention at least a few of them by name. We would like to thank:

Professor Dr. Lothar J. Seiwert for his foreword, but also for his ideas and critical support.

Tiki Küstenmacher, the best cartoonist we know. We are very glad that he has illustrated this book.

René Halbach for his detailed research work and patient gathering of first-class ideas.

Paul Donders, who is a pioneering thinker in the field of life and career planning and has allowed us to use his workshop on "What motivates me?"

Friedbert Gay, who markets the best personal development instrument in the German-speaking countries, the DISC Personal Profile System.

Traudel Knoblauch, our meticulous first reader, who subjected the manuscript to a thoroughgoing critical examination.

Our many seminar **participants,** who have helped us to identify the questions that are truly relevant and find practical answers to them.

Our editor at Campus Verlag, **Christiane Kramer,** whose optimism and enthusiasm for this project have been enduring sources of fresh motivation.

Campus Verlag, one of the most respected German business publishing houses, which recognized the importance and potential of this topic even in difficult economic times.

Jörg Knoblauch
(knoblauch@tempus.de)

Johannes Hüger
(johannes@hueger.net)

Marcus Mockler
(trainer@marcus-mockler.de)

List of the workshops

Further reading

Buford, Bob, *Halftime: Changing Your Life from Success to Significance*. Michigan, Zondervan, 2000

Chapman, Gary, *The Five Love Languages: How to Express Heartfelt Commitment to Your Mate*. Chicago, Moody Publishers, 1996

Covey, Stephen R., *The 7 Habits of Highly Effective People: Powerful Lessons in Personal Changes*. New York, Free Press, 2004

Csikszentmihalyi, Mihaly, *Flow: The Psychology of Happiness*. London, Rider, 1992

Donders, Paul Ch., *Kreative Lebensplanung* [A Creative Plan for Life]. Asslar, Gerth Medien, 2000

Gruen, Anselm, *Building Self-Esteem: The Christian Dimension*. New York, The Crossroad Publishing Company, 2000

Peter, Laurence Johnston, *The Peter Principle: Why Things Always Go Wrong*. New York, William Morrow and Co. Inc., 1969

Seiwert, Professor Dr. Lothar J., *How to Simplify Your Life: Seven Practical Steps to Letting Go of Your Burdens and Living a Happier Life*. New York, McGraw-Hill, 2004

Professor Jörg W. Knoblauch, born 1949, is the managing director of time-management specialists tempus and was awarded a Ludwig Erhard Prize for "excellence in competition" in 2002. He has published many successful books.

Johannes Hüger, born 1964, has worked as a management consultant and coach for many years and provides seminars on life and career planning.

Marcus Mockler, born 1965, is a journalist, trainer and coach specializing in communication, client-orientation and career planning.